Rayner Winterbotham

The Kingdom of Heaven

Here and hereafter

Rayner Winterbotham

The Kingdom of Heaven
Here and hereafter

ISBN/EAN: 9783337183745

Printed in Europe, USA, Canada, Australia, Japan

Cover: Foto ©Lupo / pixelio.de

More available books at **www.hansebooks.com**

THE

KINGDOM OF HEAVEN

HERE AND HEREAFTER

BY

RAYNER WINTERBOTHAM, M.A., LL.B., B.Sc.

CANON OF S. MARY'S CATHEDRAL, EDINBURGH

NEW YORK

THE MACMILLAN COMPANY

1898

CONTENTS

		PAGE
I.	THE KINGDOM OF HEAVEN	1
II.	THE PARABLE OF THE SOWER; OR, OF THE GOOD SEED	14
III.	THE PARABLE OF THE TARES OF THE FIELD	33
IV.	THE PARABLE OF THE MUSTARD SEED	52
V.	THE PARABLE OF THE LEAVEN	70
VI.	THE PARABLE OF THE HID TREASURE	77
VII.	THE PARABLE OF THE PEARL OF GREAT PRICE	90
VIII.	THE PARABLE OF THE DRAG-NET	103
IX.	THE PARABLE OF THE UNMERCIFUL SERVANT	111
X.	THE PARABLE OF THE LABOURERS	121
XI.	THE TWO PARABLES OF THE VINEYARD	129
XII.	THE PARABLE OF THE KING'S SUPPER	137
XIII.	THE THREE PARABLES OF ST. MATTHEW XXV.	145
XIV.	THE PARABLE OF THE TEN VIRGINS	166
XV.	THE PARABLE OF THE TALENTS	174
XVI.	THE PARABLE OF THE SHEEP AND GOATS	181

EXCURSUS

I.	ON SOME SAYINGS ABOUT THE KINGDOM OF HEAVEN	219
II.	ON SUFFERING AS A NOTE OF THE KINGDOM OF HEAVEN	234
III.	ON THE DESTINY OF THE LOST	241
IV.	UPON THE CIRCUMSCRIBED CHARACTER OF "THE KINGDOM" IN OUR LORD'S TEACHING	258

PREFACE

IN the following pages will be found an attempt to estimate once more our Lord's teaching about the Kingdom of Heaven. It is an arduous undertaking, in which any large measure of success can scarcely be looked for. But the present time offers some advantages which may seem to warrant the taking it in hand. We have shaken ourselves clear of certain conventional ways of treating our Lord's discourses which greatly spoilt their effectiveness and even obscured their meaning. We do not in the least desire to treat the Bible like any other book, or to rank our Lord with other Teachers of mankind. But we see quite clearly that being made Man, and speaking to His hearers in their own language, it was of necessity that He should so order His words as to produce the effect which He desired upon their minds. He spoke indeed as never man spake, but all the same He spoke as Man to men. He used a style which was distinctively Eastern, constantly figurative, not infrequently hyperbolical. Parables, proverbial sayings, figures of speech, prophetical formulas adapted from the Old Testament, were constantly on His lips. To object to this fact, as if it were in any conceivable sense derogatory or surprising, would only be to object to His being Incarnate when and where He was. To ignore this fact in interpreting His language, is to set aside the Will of God for one's private fancies. It pleased the Father that the Incarnate Word should think the thoughts and speak the language of a Jew of Palestine nineteen centuries ago. Given the Incarnation, nothing else indeed was possible. The clearest recognition of this fact does not diminish in the least from the reverence due to our Lord's words. On the contrary it adds to that reverence because it makes it more intelligent. But it does affect our interpretation of those words, when we understand that they are very far removed in literary character from the ordinary prose of modern Western life. It is a fact that our Lord desired and designed to impress upon the minds of His followers certain great ideas connected with His Kingdom. It is a fact that He had to use whatever language was then and there best adapted (or most available) for producing the desired effect. It is a fact that He actually used the language of the Prophet and the Poet, not that of the essayist or annalist, not that of the modern moralist or preacher. It is only when we recognize these facts that we can contemplate our Lord's teaching in anything like the true light. It is only when we recognize the limitations which our Lord set upon His teaching, when we cease to demand of Him definite predictions and dogmatic utterances, that our minds become really open to the splendid effectiveness of that teaching. There never was anything like it—save here and there when His Spirit spake by the Prophets of Israel. There never will be anything like it again. To treat it in the hopelessly prosaic and pedantic spirit in which it has been so often treated is (with the best intentions) to do Him a dreadful wrong. If anyone thinks the following pages chargeable with too much freedom of treatment, or with too wide departure from conventional ideas as to what our Lord *must* have meant, he is only asked to weigh each case on its merits, and to credit the author with as devout a reverence for the Incarnate Word as he has himself. It is agreed that it is not in all cases easy to know what our Lord really meant. It is agreed that it has always been an open question (and a question very ill understood by many) how far the elements of poetry and of figure and of picture-language enter into our Lord's discourse. If the author is convinced that these elements are in fact far larger and more extensive than is generally allowed, he may be wrong—but he is not therefore to be accused of want of reverence or want of faith. Nothing is further from his mind than to take up a negative attitude towards our Lord's teaching. If on the contrary he shall have done anything to bring out the magnificent and astonishing effectiveness of that teaching, and to free it from entanglements of misunderstanding, then his object will have been gained. The effort is probably worth very little : whatever it *is* worth, it is offered to HIM.

THE KINGDOM OF HEAVEN HERE AND HEREAFTER

I.

THE KINGDOM OF HEAVEN

THERE is a very marked tendency in the present day to get back to our Lord's own teaching on matters of religion. This need not be either doubted or deplored. The tendency may itself take an exaggerated form, like every movement which is largely prompted by hostility to established modes of thinking. It is in point of fact often completely vitiated by prejudice and dislike : but in itself the tendency is hopeful. It is sufficiently evident that in many ways a great deal has been read into the Master's teaching which does not belong to it. It is natural and right that those who revere Him most should wish to strip off these accretions, and to realize as distinctly as possible what He Himself really taught about religion. In order to share this wish, it is not at all necessary to set up the authority of the Master in any kind of opposition against the authority of the apostles to whom He promised the gift of the

B

Spirit to guide them into all truth : or against the
authority of the Church which is the pillar and
ground of the truth. Theoretically, there *can* be no
such opposition, for then would the Spirit and the
truth be divided against itself. Practically, whatever
opposition may appear will fall to be explained by
some mistake on our part. We have misread the
Apostles, or misjudged the voice of the Church. We
may leave that for the present, convinced that no
true development of Christian teaching (whatever its
degree of inspiration) can gainsay the teaching of
the Master or be (in any sense) inconsistent with it.
It is true then that in point of fact the appeal is
constantly being made to what our Lord taught on
certain subjects ; it is certainly lawful to ask ourselves what that teaching really comes to. And this
may be especially asserted with regard to a subject
which He made peculiarly His own, and as it were
reserved for His own explication. Everyone knows
that He spoke very often about the Kingdom of
Heaven, that it was a favourite topic of His, that He
chose to dwell upon it in His public teaching in a
very emphatic way, that it commended itself to Him
as a heading or title under which He could most
conveniently and profitably arrange His teachings
concerning those things which it most concerned us
to understand. It was His mission to proclaim, to
found, that Kingdom. It was the Kingdom which
interested Him, and in which He sought to interest
us. It certainly represented something very real and
practical to Him, and yet so inclusive that whatever
was not of it was nothing worth. If the phrase

" Kingdom of Heaven " called up in our minds what it called up in *His*—nothing more and nothing less —we should be wise indeed! It is, however, evident that to this wisdom there is no short cut. To this particular phrase there is no paraphrase, no precise equivalent in any language. No doubt the phrase itself implies something. It takes for granted the fact that the world *is* in some sense alienated from God. It takes for granted that amidst this general alienation there *is* a process of recovery which has God for its author ; a limited sphere within which He is working in a peculiar way, ruling and overruling, to bring men back to Him. So we cannot doubt that in the Divine thought this Kingdom has an absolute unity and identity. In human thought and speech, however, it is far otherwise. The moment we look at our Lord's teaching about the Kingdom we are struck with the fact that it is extraordinarily varied and discursive. We are confronted with a number of outline sketches so diverse one from another as to have almost nothing in common. Our first difficulty is to conceive how similitudes so apparently inconsistent can be true likenesses of the same divine institution. Our first lesson is one of wide-mindedness. It is indeed possible that as we go on we shall perceive some sort of unity, rising through the partial and manifold to the one and the complete. It is also possible that this is not to be realized here and now. At any rate we must be content with any amount of seeming incongruity to start with, and refuse to be tempted by that forced exegesis which has for its aim at any cost to "reconcile" scripture with scripture, or scripture as it is with our conception of scripture as it ought to be. A bitter experience has taught us both what this kind of treatment can do, and what it cannot do. On the face of things it is omnipotent. It is always possible by means of glosses and explanations to put such a face upon any scripture as that it shall at least be dumb and not give the lie to our reading of any other scripture. But in the end it is impotent. It never satisfies people who think. The written record remains, infinitely patient indeed of arbitrary treatment and violence, but always bearing its own witness, and always finding some ears open to that witness. Our first lesson then is one of comprehensiveness. The Kingdom of Heaven in our Lord's presentation of it is like unto a dozen different things —so different that theology can find no common measure for them. Yet we cannot doubt that the truth of the Kingdom is to be found not in the exclusive contemplation of any one or two of these aspects, but in giving due place and full importance to every aspect in its turn. There are those who are in favour of very short formulas in religion : they cannot be in harmony with our Lord's teaching in the Gospels. There are those who insist much upon the simplicity of the Gospel. They are right in their way, but they need to recognize that our Lord's teaching was simple because each picture that He held up was so clear and so incisive, not at all because the pictures were the same or were even alike. Simplicity must never be confounded with narrowness of view, or with failure to grasp the

many co-ordinate and complemental elements in
our Lord's teaching, and in the teaching of scripture
generally. If that teaching had been "simple" in
the sense often claimed for it, He would doubtless
have found one parable in which He might express
the truth of the Kingdom. It is evident that He
could not do this: the many-sidedness of the Kingdom forbade it. The parables of the Kingdom are
like pictures or photographs of some great edifice
taken from points of view so various that they
bear almost no resemblance to one another. Any
one or two, taken apart from the rest, would be
erroneous because fatally incomplete. And yet each
is absolutely true in itself, and its truth is substantiated by Christian history and Christian experience, so far as these have gone. What we have
do do, therefore, if we wish to understand the Kingdom of Heaven as our Lord thought of it, is to take
all these parables as they are, to place ourselves at
their varying standpoints, and to realize that aspect
of the Kingdom which is presented in each.

Of set parables concerning the Kingdom of
Heaven there are fourteen in St. Matthew, and
one (additional) in St. Mark. Pre-eminent amongst
these are the two great series of seven parables in
St. Matthew xiii., and of three in St. Matthew xxv.
Besides these there is a large number of sayings
about the kingdom, especially in St. Luke, which are
of the greatest importance. It must be evident to
every careful reader that the Gospels are full of
sayings which only need working up in order to be
called parables. They are the raw material of

parable. They are pregnant sayings, illustrations, similitudes, which the evangelists in some cases actually call parables (as in St. Luke v. 36, St. Mark xiii. 28), but which are not in fact elaborated into the word-picture to which *we* restrict the name. For affirming the distinctive features of the Kingdom they may be equally important, though not nearly so striking. We must try not to lose sight of these, while we give chief attention to the two great groups of parables in St. Matthew's Gospel. It may indeed be argued that the former of these groups is an artificial one, that they have only been gathered together here for convenience. But our Lord's question in St. Matthew xiii. 51, "Have ye understood *all* these things?" seems to imply that all these parables belong together, and need to be taken in connection with one another in order to be properly understood. Of course we cannot take the apostles' answer, "Yea, Lord," as representing the fact. It measured their ignorance rather than their knowledge—their ignorance of all the wisdom which lies within these parables, which nineteen centuries have failed to exhaust. But all the same our Lord's words serve to gather together all these parables of the Kingdom, and to present them to us as an object of devout study in their unity as well as in their variety.

Before taking up the detailed examination of these parables, however, it will be well to point out what the time relations of the Kingdom of Heaven are, in our Lord's use of the phrase. It has relations with past, present, and future. Where, for instance, our

Lord says that "the children of the Kingdom shall be cast out,"[1] it is manifest from the context that He is speaking of Jews, who by reason of their privileged position under the old dispensation might naturally claim the freedom of the Kingdom more than any others. Nor does He exactly disallow that claim. Abraham and Isaac and Jacob *do* belong to the Kingdom, and are prominent in it.[2] But these "sons of the Kingdom," as they are by hereditary right, must nevertheless be excluded since they have no real congruity with it. The Kingdom of which our Lord thought had therefore a sort of preliminary (or anticipatory) and partial existence in the past, in that Old Testament economy which He came at once to fulfil and to supersede.

But it is certain that this existence of the Kingdom in the past has but a small and casual place in our Lord's teaching, and it is only necessary to point it out for the sake of completeness. Generally speaking He is at pains to emphasize the fact that the Kingdom has only come with Himself, and is only now available. Even John the Baptist, to whom He pays so high a tribute of praise, is not (properly speaking) within the Kingdom.[3] Close as he stands to the Messiah, he does not himself belong to the Christian order of things, and so remains inferior to many commonplace people in point of position and privilege. To be fairly within the Kingdom of Heaven it is not enough to be even the forerunner of our Lord: one must be distinctly a follower of His. Habitually our Lord speaks of the Kingdom

[1] Matt. viii. 12.   [2] *Ibid.* 11.   [3] Matt. xi. 11.

in the present tense; "no doubt the Kingdom of
God is come upon you"; "the Kingdom of God is
within you" (or perhaps "among you").[1]   That
manner of speech may be said to be usual with
Him. But at the same time He speaks of it as
future, and that emphatically. Thus He does not
encourage the popular idea that "the Kingdom of
God should immediately appear,"[2] and He teaches
the disciples to pray "Thy Kingdom come."[3] Concerning some of them He asserts that they "shall
not taste of death until they see the Kingdom of
God,"[4] and He tells the twelve at the Last Supper
that He "will not drink from henceforth of the fruit
of the vine, until the Kingdom of God shall come."[5]
It is obvious that this emphatic reference to the
future does not *in itself* raise any difficulty, any
more than that other and slighter reference to the
past. If, as we should naturally suppose, the Kingdom is essentially a state of things introduced into
the world by our Lord, it would necessarily have its
more or less shadowy anticipations in the past; still
more necessarily its historical developments in the
future. The Jewish "children of the Kingdom" did
really possess the earthly counterpart of the heavenly
reality of that Kingdom. When we pray "Thy
Kingdom come," we mean "come in its perfect
fulness." Those who were to survive (no doubt
very unexpectedly and by the singular favour of
God) to "see the Kingdom of God," were (as St.

---

[1] Luke xvii. 21.   [2] Luke xix. 11.
[3] Matt. vi. 10 ; Luke ix. 2.   [4] Luke ix. 27.
[5] Luke xxii. 18.

Mark indeed expresses it, ix. 1) to "see the Kingdom of God come *with power*," *i.e.*, in some startling
development of its boundless influence for good.
Those who are to drink the cup of blessing new
with their Lord in the Kingdom of God will drink
it (whatever that may mean) "in the regeneration,"
i.e., in the age to come when the Kingdom shall
have reached its final stage of absolute perfection.
There is nothing whatever arbitrary in this, because
the coming of the Kingdom is so often and so clearly
thought of as being gradual and progressive.   In the
one parable peculiar to St. Mark (iv. 26-9) there is
no other point than this.   Gradually, and even insensibly, while men pursue their ordinary avocations,
and the earth swings round and round upon its axis,
the seed is growing and ripening towards maturity.
When that maturity *is* finally reached, there will be
no delay in reaping the fruits ; but until that hour is
come it will just go on growing, ripening, developing,
maturing, or by whatever other word one may choose
to describe the evolution of the Kingdom.   No one
has ever made anything else of the parable.   But in
this simple and obvious sense it is perfect.   There
are moments in the growth of the corn when men
remark with a certain surprise on the change which
has come over its appearance.   As a rule they pay
no heed to it.   But it goes on growing none the faster
for their regard, and none the slower for their dis-
regard.   So is the Kingdom of God, always past
(since He "left not Himself without witness from
the beginning"[1]), always present (since "here and

[1] Acts xiv. 17.

now" is the law of man's responsibility), always future (since "the Kingdom" is also "the patience of Jesus Christ"[1]).

Moreover it is entirely after our Lord's manner to use words and phrases with a singular absoluteness and absence of qualification, leaving it to His hearers to explain them by the context, or to modify them by complemental sayings. That is the case in things far more important and difficult than time-relations. It should not then (and *would* not, apart from pre-conceived theories) cause us any surprise, or give us any trouble, if we find Him speaking simply and absolutely of "the Kingdom," whether He was at the moment thinking of it as past, present, or future, in its anticipation, in its essential character, or in its development. This being so, it is clear that in considering any particular parable of the Kingdom we must carefully interrogate Christian history as to any light which that history can throw upon it, since, every distinctive feature of the Kingdom must leave unmistakable marks upon the course of events. No one doubts that Christianity has profoundly affected the progress of affairs from the first, and no one doubts that the Kingdom of Heaven stands in close relationship to what we call Christianity, although much which is included under that name is not of the Kingdom. Christian history therefore should help us very much, both positively by suggesting the true line of interpretation, and negatively by barring the false. We need, however, to rely upon broad and general views of history only, and not

[1] Rev. i. 9.

upon narrow or detailed applications. It is not necessary to ask whether our Lord had before His mind the whole sequence of the future of this world. It is enough to know (as we really *may* know for certain) that if He had He never made the slightest use of that knowledge. Beyond the destruction of Jerusalem (so often depicted by the prophets of Israel) He never foretold one single event in history, and even those few prognostications that He made of the fate which awaited some of His disciples[1] were couched in terms of such studied vagueness that only the event could determine what they meant. This reticence was no doubt intentional, and all really reverent minds will hold it in absolute respect. Practically, our Lord predicted nothing in the way of what we call occurrences. What He did was to forecast certain lines along which His Kingdom would develop, because these lines corresponded to its essential features. It is in this respect, and only this, that we must seek for light from Christian history. To anticipate very briefly what will appear further on, it may be granted that as the parable of the sower deals primarily with the conditions of the apostolic age, so the parable of the tares is primarily concerned with such spurious imitations of Christianity as formed a very prominent feature of the second century. The parable of the mustard-seed depicts the surprisingly swift growth of Christianity as a corporate institution, while that of the leaven sets forth as clearly the far wider extension of its characteristic ideas. All that corresponds

---

[1] Matt. xx. 23 ; John xxi. 18, 22.

markedly in a broad sense to the actual course
of things, but it cannot be carried any further. We
might infer that our Lord's vision of the future did
not extend further, or pass more into detail, than
that. Such an inference would be precarious. But
we are bound to treat the parables as if it were true.
Whatever limits He Himself imposed upon His
utterances we must absolutely respect : and when
history shows clearly that such limits existed, we
must conclude that He Himself imposed them.
That is the only reasonable or reverent line to take,
even if it cut the ground from beneath a vast edifice
of assertion or of speculation. To this limited use
of Christian history may be added an almost unlimited use of Christian experience, since the Kingdom fulfils and unfolds itself in and for the individual
quite as much as in and for the community. The
parables, *e.g.*, of the hid treasure and of the pearl
are obviously to be expounded from the records of
the inner life : like certain other parables of the
Kingdom, they absolutely decline to concern themselves with Christians in general, they will only take
men one by one in the most personal way possible.

One more "foreword." No attempt will be made
to go behind the Gospel narratives. They will be
taken as they stand. And this, not out of any
desire to judge others or to limit their liberty, but
out of conviction that the path in that direction leads
to nothing. If a hundred men started off to cross a
level and featureless moorland on a dark and wind-
less night, when the moon did not shine, and the few
stars visible could not be recognized, the value of

their explorations would be nil. Their devious course until the dawn would be determined only by the action and reaction of the unimportant and superficial inequalities of the surface upon their personal idiosyncrasies. No conceivable value would attach to the result. Equally useless, because equally casual and unaccountable, is the blind guessing of those who wish to go behind the Gospels. Doubtless they form opinions, but they have not any data to form them on. The Gospels are in possession. They have been in possession from a date which every fresh discovery tends to put nearer and nearer to the apostolic days. No one who really believes in the love and wisdom of the Father of our Lord Jesus Christ can lightly believe that the Gospels are not authentic for all practical purposes.

II.

THE PARABLE OF THE SOWER;
OR, OF THE GOOD SEED

St. Matt. xiii. 3-8.

Behold, a sower went forth to sow: And when he sowed some *seeds* fell by the way side, and the fowls came and devoured them up: Some fell upon stony places, where they had not much earth: and forthwith they sprung up, because they had no deepness of earth: And when the sun was up, they were scorched: and because they had no root, they withered away. And some fell among thorns; and the thorns sprung up, and choked them: But other fell into good ground, and brought forth fruit, some an hundredfold, some sixtyfold, some thirtyfold.

St. Mark iv. 3-8

Hearken; behold, there went out a sower to sow: And it came to pass, as he sowed, some fell by the way side, and the fowls of the air came and devoured it up. And some fell on stony ground, where it had not much earth; and immediately it sprang up, because it had no depth of earth: But when the sun was up, it was scorched; and because it had no root, it withered away. And some fell among thorns, and the thorns grew up and choked it, and it yielded no fruit. And other fell on good ground, and did yield fruit that sprang up and increased, and brought forth, some thirty, and some sixty, and some an hundred.

St. Luke viii. 5-8.

A sower went out to sow his seed: and as he sowed, some fell by the way side; and it was trodden down, and the fowls of the air devoured it. And some fell upon a rock; and as soon as it was sprung up, it withered away, because it lacked moisture. And some fell among thorns; and the thorns sprang up with it, and choked it. And other fell on good ground, and sprang up, and bare fruit an hundredfold.

14

THE PARABLE OF THE SOWER 15

St. Matt. xiii. 18-23.

Hear ye therefore the parable of the sower. When any one heareth the word of the kingdom, and understandeth *it* not, then cometh the wicked *one*, and catcheth away that which was sown in his heart. This is he which received seed by the way side. But he that received the seed into stony places, the same is he that heareth the word, and anon with joy receiveth it : Yet hath he not root in himself, but dureth for a while: for when tribulation or persecution ariseth because of the word, by and by he is offended. He also that received seed among the thorns is he that heareth the word; and the care of this world, and the deceitfulness of riches, choke the word, and he becometh unfruitful. But he that received seed into the good ground is he that heareth the

St. Mark iv. 14-20.

The sower soweth the word. And these are they by the way side, where the word is sown; but when they have heard, Satan cometh immediately, and taketh away the word that was sown in their hearts. And these are they likewise which are sown on stony ground ; who, when they have heard the word, immediately receive it with gladness ; and have no root in themselves, and so endure but for a time : afterward, when affliction or persecution ariseth for the word's sake, immediately they are offended. And these are they which are sown among thorns; such as hear the word. And the cares of this world, and the deceitfulness of riches, and the lusts of other things entering in, choke the word, and it becometh unfruitful. And these are they which are sown on good ground; such as hear the

St. Luke viii. 11-15.

Now the parable is this : The seed is the word of God. Those by the way side are they that hear ; then cometh the devil, and taketh away the word out of their hearts, lest they should believe and be saved. They on the rock *are they*, which, when they hear, receive the word with joy; and these have no root, which for a while believe, and in time of temptation fall away. And that which fell among thorns are they, which, when they have heard, go forth, and are choked with cares and riches and pleasures of *this* life, and bring no fruit to perfection. But that on the good ground are they, which in an honest and good heart, having heard the word, keep *it*, and bring forth fruit with patience.

St. Matt. xiii. 18-23.	*St. Mark* iv. 14-20.
word, and under-standeth *it*; which also beareth fruit, and bringeth forth, some an hundredfold, some sixty, some thirty.	word, and receive *it*, and bring forth fruit, some thirtyfold, some sixty, and some an hundred.

THE PARABLE OF
THE GOOD SEED GROWING SECRETLY
St. Mark iv. 26-29.

And he said, So is the kingdom of God, as if a man should cast seed into the ground; and should sleep, and rise night and day, and the seed should spring and grow up, he knoweth not how. For the earth bringeth forth fruit of herself; first the blade, then the ear, after that the full corn in the ear. But when the fruit is ripe immediately he putteth in the sickle, because the harvest is come.

THAT the first and foremost of all agricultural operations should have furnished the Saviour with much of the imagery of His parables is natural enough. The operation itself was familiar to everybody, and almost equally familiar were many of the sentiments and applications which readily suggest themselves. That which comes of the sowing—the fields of harvest—is so utterly unlike the sowing, so far away, and yet so confidently expected. And side by side with the general certainty of harvest—of the special harvest which the sowing warrants—lies the extraordinary uncertainty of the event in the case of the particular plant or field.

There are four parables of sowing which concern the Kingdom of Heaven. That of the mustard seed, however, we may put aside, because it only belongs to this group in appearance. It is in fact a story, not of the sower, but of the gardener, and has an entirely different significance. There remain as true parables of sowing the first two in St. Matthew xiii., and the one in St. Mark iv. 26-29. This last has been already considered. Its one point—so very simple, and yet of such profound interest—is the silent persistent growth, unhastening, unhindered, of Christian influences, towards the inevitable hour of perfect ripeness. There is in it a suggestion that these influences may seem to be left strangely to themselves, as if they needed no supervision. And that is true in this respect, that they are vital influences and are bound to go on growing and maturing according to the law of development which belongs to their nature. They may be the better for man's solicitude, but they do not depend upon it.

The parable which governs the others—which rules the interpretation of them—is undoubtedly that commonly called " the parable of the sower." This is, however, a misnomer, because nothing whatever turns upon the personality of him that bears the seed. In the parable, as in real life, this is unimportant. When the Revised Version rightly enough substitutes " *the* sower " for " *a* sower," it nevertheless puts the reader on a wrong track. " The sower " is simply the man who, as a matter of fact, is employed in this humble task. It may be indeed our Lord ; it may be St. Peter or St. John ; it may as well be Judas ; St. Paul—or those who preached Christ even of envy and strife. What matters is not the sower, but the seed. No doubt there is a skill and carefulness in sowing ; but that is not any part of the

c

parable. It is the seed upon which everything turns from the first, and after that it is the strange and varied fortunes of that seed, with which the sower has nothing to do. It will be as well to remember that, in an age which takes an unwearied delight in discussing and comparing the personal characteristics and peculiarities of preachers.

Now the seed is "the word" (St. Mark), "the word of the Kingdom" (St. Matthew), "the word of God" (St. Luke). By these expressions is signified no doubt that teaching about divine and eternal things which is proper and (for the most part) peculiar to Christianity. It cannot possibly be doubted that our Lord thought of His own teaching—the substance of which is recorded in the Gospels—as the word of God. "My mother and My brethren are these *which hear the word of God*, and do it." He never showed the slightest consciousness that the seed which He sowed as the word of God was an imperfectly-developed seed, having no vitality, no living principle in itself. It is certain that the word of God as preached by the Apostles never discarded, never superseded, any part of our Lord's personal teaching. In one notable instance indeed, that of St. James, it simply reproduced it. You understand the Epistle of St. James only when you hear in it just the echoes of the old Galilean teaching of the Son of Man in those blessed days of His visible presence. Just thus, we may say to ourselves, had the Master spoken on some well-remembered occasion in Bethsaida or in Capernaum, turning as He spoke now to the simple country folk, now to the Scribes and Pharisees who came down from Jerusalem.

On the other hand St. Paul expressly identifies the word of God with "the word of the Cross,"[1] and this raises questions which have to be faced. What does the Apostle mean by this expression ὁ λόγος τοῦ Σταυροῦ, and in what precise relation does it stand to the word of the Kingdom as preached by our Lord? It may be as well to glance first of all at an explanation which is worthless enough in itself, but is worth a good deal as a specimen of its kind. Not long ago a fragment of the "Gospel according to Peter" was discovered, and in it occurs the story of what we may call the Resurrection of the Cross. On the third day, very early, a cross of supernatural size is seen to issue from the sepulchre, escorted by two gigantic angels. It has occurred to someone to assert that when St. Paul uses the expression ὁ λόγος τοῦ Σταυροῦ, he refers to this "story of the Cross," this ridiculous legend. It is enough for anybody who knows his Bible to recall the sayings of St. Paul about the Cross, how evidently spiritual and mystical the Cross was to him, how entirely the mere physical facts and circumstances of the Crucifixion sank into insignificance as compared with the enormous issues of spiritual religion which lay behind and beneath the Crucifixion. It is not enough to say that the assertion was false. It is clear that it could not have been made by anyone who had the least sympathy with or insight into the thoughts and feelings of St.

[1] I Cor. i. 18, R.V.; the A.V. "preaching of the Cross" is absolutely unwarrantable.

Paul as manifested in his letters. Even a very limited insight, and that purely intellectual, would have saved a man from making such a stupid blunder. But it is only a rather crass specimen of a multitude of assertions which are constantly being made about the origins of Christianity, wildly improbable guesses based upon nothing but an eager and sometimes virulent dislike of the common belief, yet often accepted for no better reason than that they are at once surprising and confident.

When St. Paul identifies the word of God with the word of the Cross, he means no doubt that in his preaching Christ *crucified* was the central figure. One knows that it was so. "O foolish Galatians," he cries, " who did bewitch you, before whose eyes Jesus Christ was openly set forth, crucified?"[1] "Openly set forth" is a lame translation. Bishop Lightfoot renders it "placarded," and no doubt rightly. No one will suspect for an instant that the Apostle stuck up flaming "posters" of the Crucifixion. Nothing is more impossible. But he uses the word which other people used for the posting up of public decrees and notices. He had so preached Christ crucified that the picture of the dying Saviour lived before the mind's eye of the Galatians. As they listened they were again and again transported to Calvary, and beheld the dying of the Lord Jesus. That is clear. But we cannot read St. Paul's letters and doubt that the "word of the Cross" means more than that to him. "The

[1] Gal. iii. 1.

Cross" is to him the verbal symbol, not only of a crucified Saviour, but of a crucified self. By it he is crucified to the world and the world to him. He is constantly assuming that all good Christians died, were crucified, with Christ in a very real sense. Doubtless there is something mystical in this teaching which it passes man's wit to explain, which only faith can appropriate and experience make clear. But yet no one doubts that this truth has a moral or ethical side of the gravest import. The "word of the Cross" means also the teaching (so inextricably mixed up by the Apostle with the teaching about the atoning Death) that all who will be saved by Christ must die to sin and die to self, and rise to a new life of unselfishness and devotion. Now here we see in a moment that St. Paul's word of the Cross is our Lord's word of the Kingdom. This was historically the first meaning of the Cross. As our Saviour Himself speaks of it, it is *we* who are to take it up and follow Him. "He that taketh not his Cross," He said, "is not worthy of Me."[1] Surprising, if we were not so used to it, that He speaks of the Cross for *us* before He speaks of the Cross for Himself! No possible "return to the Cross" can ever alter that fact, nor must we shrink from honestly giving full value to it. The word of God in the mouth of the Master and in the mouth of the Apostle was "good seed," seed which was fitted by its inherent power of life to spring up and bring forth fruit for the harvest of eternity. It was good seed, because it contained within itself

[1] Matt. x. 38.

the word of the Cross, the Cross for all men, the Cross as an all-embracing principle of self-sacrifice and self-renunciation, a principle which was in the supreme sense illustrated, confirmed, established by the Death at Calvary. We need not think that this is the last word about the Atonement. Far from it. That last word will never be spoken. When the Son of God delivers Himself up to death for us men and for our salvation, the effects of it will be so prodigious, the very meaning of it so far beyond our powers of thought, that we shall never think we have exhausted that meaning, or wish to set limits to those effects. Moreover, we are per-fectly aware that our Lord could only speak in hints and dark sayings about His approaching Passion. Still it remains true that if we seek for that which is common to the teaching of Christ and of St. Paul, we find it above all in two elements. The first is the extraordinary and (upon any but the Christian theory) inexplicable prominence given to the Person of our Lord. In the Gospels quite as much as the Epistles it is He that is evermore proposed to men, not merely as their Exemplar and Teacher, but as the supreme object of their loyalty, devotion, obedience, worship. The second is " the Cross " in the broad sense above referred to.

In the Gospels then we have Christ and the Cross. In the Epistles Christ and *His* Cross, because now He has not only perfectly illustrated, but adequately fulfilled this eternal and Divine principle, and made the Cross His own for ever. But Christ and the Cross, whether the two thoughts have as yet imperfectly united, or whether they have absolutely coalesced, make up the vital principle in the good seed.   It remains then to affirm that Christ and *His* Cross must not abolish Christ and *the* Cross, for they are not contrary the one to the other.   People have wondered why the "word of the Cross" seemed to have lost its power, and did not see that its power was gone because there was no Cross in it for him that preached or for them that heard.   Men go forth to the heathen and say, "The Son of God died for you; believe on Him and all will be well with you"; and they are surprised that the message falls almost flat, and that they get no converts but such as they pay for one way or another.   That is not the word of the Cross as our Lord taught it, or St. Paul.   In our Lord's mouth it was, "He that taketh not his cross, and followeth after Me, is not worthy of Me."[1]   In St. Paul's, "I die daily";[2] "I am crucified with Christ";[3] "If we died with Him, we shall also live with Him."[4]   To preach Christ without self-sacrifice and self-devotion, without a veritable surrender of what the natural man loves and longs for, is a blunder so fatal that it takes all the life out of it.   "The word of the Cross" means of course all the love of Christ crucified *for* us, but it means also all the love of Christ crucified *in* us.   It means the fundamental truth so incisively taught—so paradoxically taught even—by the Master, that you must lose your life (or soul) in order to gain it.   How amazing it is, by the way, that this

---

[1] Matt. x. 38.   [2] I Cor. xv. 31.
[3] Gal. ii. 20.   [4] Rom. vi. 8.

great saying in St. Matthew xvi. 25, 26 should have been utterly changed and corrupted for so many millions of English-speaking Christians ever since the Reformation! When our translators rendered the same Greek word by "life" in verse 25, and by "soul" in verse 26, they did not *mean* to deal dishonestly with the word of God; but what they did was absolutely unwarrantable, and has been disastrous beyond expression. If there is one thing in religion of which the ordinary English Bible-reader is persuaded, it is this, that our Lord urges upon him the supreme duty of saving his "soul," even (if needs be) at the expense of his "life." If one tells him that "life" and "soul," as our Lord uses the word, are identical—that he must be willing and ready to lose his soul, his very and eternal self, in order to save it—he only wonders from what source such pestilent folly can proceed. Yet the more the saying is considered, the more hopelessly plain it is that all the centuries of teaching, all the millions of sermons founded upon this celebrated text in the Authorised Version, have been clean contrary to our Lord's meaning. Verse 26 has for its sole purpose to aggravate (so to speak) the awful cost of the sacrifice demanded in verse 25. That which a man calls his "life" or "soul" is his supreme possession, beside which all other possible belongings sink into insignificance; yet it is precisely *this* which a man must be prepared to surrender, to suffer the total loss of, if he is (in the Divine sense) to gain it. When St. Paul says (and he evidently means it) that he could wish that he himself were anathema from Christ for the sake of his Jewish brethren,[1] we understand at once that he had entered into the full and true meaning of this word of the Kingdom which he so justly calls the word of the Cross. You *must* give up—not by way of a commercial bargain, as for value received, but joyfully and without reservation—all your own life, with all its desires and ambitions and aggrandizements; and then the true eternal life will be yours. The "word of the Cross" means that for the man himself it is better to fail than to succeed, better to be despised than to be highly esteemed, better to be poor than to be rich, better to die than to live. All this (and more of the same kind) did "the Cross" imply for those who first heard of it, Jews or Greeks. And those who (very naturally) hated all this and spoke against it, and evaded it even when attracted by other aspects of Christianity, were "the enemies of the Cross of Christ,"[2] as St. Paul would warn us even with tears, so sorry is he for their fatal error. It is absolutely clear from the context (Phil. iii. 17–21) that their dislike to the Cross was not in the least theological, but altogether moral and ethical. It was not any dogma of the atonement that alienated them, but the demand that they should be content to lose their "life" of eating and drinking and enjoying themselves.

The good seed is the word of the Kingdom, the word of the Cross. Wherever it is sown it will spring up with more or less of permanent result. It may seem a strange thing to say, but it is true,

---

[1] Rom. ix. 3.   [2] Phil. iii. 18.

that the astonishing success of the Salvation Army
is due to precisely the same cause as that of so many
Roman Catholic missions. The organization and
the apparatus are no doubt cleverly arranged and
adapted, but they are absolutely of the earth earthy,
and are such as our Lord would have held very
cheap. The Army succeeds because it has got the
right sort of seed to sow—the word of the Cross
for themselves and for their hearers, as well as for
Christ. Just because they offer their officers nothing
but poverty, toil, exposure, curses, blows, they get
them in crowds. The posts most coveted are those
in which there is most to suffer. Why not?
Christianity addresses itself to what is noblest in
human nature, to that latent chivalry and loyalty
which grace can restore and exalt so wonderfully.
Give men or women a chance to suffer and to die
for some great cause, some great ideal, some great
hero, and how wonderfully they respond! When
the cause is the saving of the world, when the ideal
is the Kingdom of Heaven, when the hero is the
incarnate Son of God, it would be amazing indeed
if an unquenchable enthusiasm were not evoked.
Our Lord threw Himself (humanly speaking) altogether upon the wonderful capacity for self-
sacrificing devotion which is latent in human nature.
He offered no attractions, as far as this world is
concerned, but the opportunity of giving everything
else up in order to please Him and to do good to
others. Evidently He had entire confidence that
this one attraction would draw to His side all who
were worth drawing. The word of the Kingdom

instinctively recommended itself to the "honest and good heart" just because it called for the most tremendous sacrifices, for the most complete renunciation.[1]

We all know that seed can be "sterilized" by being exposed to a certain temperature, or treated with certain acids. The seed is the word of God; but if the word be preached as a kind of glorified counsel of prudence and self-interest, if we take out of it its original appeal to the enthusiasm, the chivalry, the power of self-sacrifice which is in men, the word is sterilized, and none need wonder that it is unfruitful. The genuine seed is only *fitly* sown by those who "for the Kingdom of Heaven's sake" leave behind them all they love, make no reserves and claim no immunities, renounce all the rewards and attractions of the world; those, in fact, across whose lives are written plain the words, "having nothing, yet possessing all things." All manner of eloquence, and attractiveness, and cleverness are mere dust and rubbish as compared with this,

[1] If this seem exaggerated, let the reader refer to the difficult saying in St. Matthew xix. 12. Whatever may be the full significance of that passage, one is at least safe in saying that our Lord there speaks of the renunciation in some form of what is most prized—and innocently prized—among earthly satisfactions. This was already being done, He says, "for the Kingdom of Heaven's sake." Not for the sake of getting to Heaven—God forbid!—as though one could purchase eternal bliss by some temporal abnegations. No; but "for the Kingdom of Heaven's sake," *i.e.*, out of a pure, disinterested, devotion to the interests of Jesus Christ, of His Church and Gospel, of all that is rightly called by His name and connected with His service. It is precisely when He speaks of these renunciations that our Lord seems to be least restrained, least careful to measure His words, or to guard Himself from being misunderstood.

because this alone puts the sower in moral harmony with the seed, which is the word of the Cross. No doubt he can deliver the true message without himself responding to it. Did not Judas also preach the Kingdom of Heaven in his day? But it will not be good for him, nor in the long run effective for others.

The parable of the good seed (as we ought to call it) is principally occupied with the fortunes of the seed after it is sown—fortunes so extraordinarily diverse as to call aloud for explanation. But clearly it was not our Saviour's purpose to *explain* anything, if by that we mean a bringing to light of the underlying facts of human nature. One sees, of course, that some men are "trivial" (the word itself is derived from the beaten pathway); nothing seems to make much real impression upon them, and because it does not find any lodgment beneath the surface it is removed by any chance influence or passing interest. One sees that others are naturally shallow, and the deepest convictions they are capable of are quickly run through and done with. Others again are so engrossed with worldly cares and so forth, that their better nature is stifled. All these differences lie upon the surface of human character, and they explain, as far as they go, the extremely different reception which actually awaits the word of the Kingdom in different quarters; but they themselves are merely noted, not in any way explained. We wish to ask of the Speaker a thousand questions. Whence do these differences of character or of temperament arise? Are they final?

Can they not be dealt with? Must those which are unfavourable always be fatal? Is there no process, *e.g.*, by which a shallow character may be deepened? Is not the Gospel intended for mankind at large? and does it not appeal to something which is in every man? Can it be true that it has, in fact, no chance of success except with such as are pre-disposed by nature to receive it? And if so, what must be held responsible for a cleavage in human nature so fundamental, so all-important? To all which the only answer is that the parable does not concern itself at all with any of these matters. It simply takes men as they are in character and temperament, and points out how the differences which actually exist affect the reception of the word. Equally hopeless it is, therefore, to enquire into the nature and origin of the " honest and good heart "[1] of which our Lord speaks. It is certain that no modern theologian would have ventured to speak of an honest and good heart as pre-existing in man before the coming of the word. He may, of course, try to explain it by pointing to the secret operation of the Spirit of God preparing certain men for faith and obedience. But there is absolutely no allusion to any such preparation in the parable. It is a fact that wherever the Gospel comes, among the heathen or the lapsed, a certain number of individuals *do* receive it with candour, with enthusiasm, with patience, because their goodness of character and disposition instinctively respond to it. It is a fact that one child, growing up unbaptized amidst heathenish

[1] Luke viii. 15.

surroundings, remains pure and true, welcomes the word of the Cross with open arms, and remains faithful unto death; while another child, most Christianly reared and tended, shows an unmistakable aversion to that word from its earliest years, and persists to the end in that aversion. It is inexplicable, but it is true; and the Saviour notes the fact quite simply, quite plainly, without any attempt to go behind it or throw any light upon it. The "honest and good heart" (the *anima naturaliter Christiana* of Tertullian) would be explained by Augustine as the result of God's arbitrary decree, by Buddha as the reward of a previous life-history. Our Saviour does not explain it at all. Nor can we. It is an absolute, an inscrutable, mystery.

Two conclusions arise naturally, and (we may venture to say) certainly, out of our investigation of this first parable of the Kingdom—conclusions which apply with more or less force to the whole series. The first is that the teaching conveyed is extraordinarily original and unexpected. There are, of course, many allusions to sowing, and to that which comes of it, in the Old Testament; but nothing there prepares us in the very least for this picture of results. The surprising variety of the results (even when there are any) is altogether peculiar, and could not possibly have been foreseen from an Old Testament point of view. Everything in the education of the disciples would dispose them to believe that the powers of the Kingdom would work uniformly and on a vast scale with little or no

reference to individual differences. All the eschatology of the prophets looks that way. But in our
Lord's parable there is the widest possible variety in
the effects actually produced. And that, although
totally unexpected, has been always and everywhere
the case. Even where the corporate, the imperial, the
catholic, conception of the Kingdom has been most
prominently asserted, the existence of this most
tremendous, most momentous, variety of results has
never been questioned. Only familiarity blinds us
to the significance of this fact.

The second, and even more widely important, consideration is this. Whilst the "parable" is the most
picturesque and most telling of all methods of
conveying truth, it is also the most strictly limited.
It conveys in the most incisive manner a single
lesson, and in every other respect it utterly refuses
to be interrogated. Probably it commended itself to
our Lord for this very reason. He evidently wished
to communicate truth very partially, very gradually,
very imperfectly—if imperfection be measured by
the desire of man to know. Nothing, *e.g.*, could be
more absolutely contrasted than the finished system
of the Schoolmen, in which every point and detail of
religion is clearly defined and settled, and the teaching of our Lord as recorded in the Gospels. They
do not only differ as the rough sketch may differ
from the finished picture: they differ in their design,
their whole conception of what the object of religious
teaching is. Obviously our Lord's intention was as
much negative as positive. Vast tracts of possible
knowledge, which human curiosity would dearly love

to explore, are left shrouded in impenetrable shadow. Partly by employing language so figurative as to defy literal acceptation, partly by using at all times the parable, which refuses to be interrogated beyond its obvious and very limited scope, He succeeded in concentrating the whole light of His revelation upon a comparatively few points which He considered of supreme importance. This consideration will need to be urged hereafter. As far as the parables of sowing are concerned, it is sufficiently recognized. Everybody knows that there are great moral problems connected with that wide diversity of results so picturesquely set forth. Everybody feels that they demand an explanation. Nobody looks to the parable for that explanation, because it is plain that beyond its own very limited scope the parable will not tell us, and was not meant to tell us, anything whatever. This is the more noteworthy because this parable is one of the few which our Lord Himself interpreted. We may say, with perfect reverence, that His interpretation adds nothing whatever to our understanding. Apparently, as far as we are concerned, its only object is to show us yet more plainly in what directions it is useless to pursue enquiries. We should have been able to interpret the good seed, the birds of the air, the thorns, the shallow soil, for ourselves ; and beyond these simple things the interpretation does not pretend to go— doubtless because the parable itself has no further scope than the one lesson involved in these.

III.

THE PARABLE OF THE TARES OF THE FIELD

St. Matthew xiii. 24–30 ; 37–43.

Another parable put he forth unto them, saying, The kingdom of heaven is likened unto a man which sowed good seed in his field : but while men slept, his enemy came and sowed tares among the wheat, and went his way. But when the blade was sprung up, and brought forth fruit, then appeared the tares also. So the servants of the householder came and said unto him, Sir, didst not thou sow good seed in thy field ? from whence then hath it tares ? He said unto them, An enemy hath done this. The servants said unto him, Wilt thou then that we go and gather them up ? But he said, Nay ; lest while ye gather up the tares, ye root up also the wheat with them. Let both grow together until the harvest : and in the time of harvest I will say to the reapers, Gather ye together first the tares, and bind them in bundles to burn them : but gather the wheat into my barn.

He answered and said unto them, He that soweth the good seed is the Son of man ; the field is the world ; the good seed are the children of the kingdom ; but the tares are the children of the wicked *one ;* the enemy that sowed them is the devil ; the harvest is the end of the world ; and the reapers are the angels. As therefore the tares are gathered and burned in the fire ; so shall it be in the end of this world. The Son of man shall send forth his angels, and they shall gather out of his kingdom all things that offend, and them which do iniquity ; and shall cast them into a furnace of fire : there shall be wailing and gnashing of teeth. Then shall the righteous shine forth as the sun in the kingdom of their Father.

"THE parable of the tares of the field"—that is what the Disciples called it,[1] and the name has clung to it. But it would be more

[1] Matt. xiii. 36.

accurate to call it the parable of the good and bad
seed, just as the first is properly called the parable of
the good seed.   If we habitually spoke of them by
these names it would be easier for us to bear in mind
the relationship between them, which is very close
indeed. For the fact is that other people can sow,
and do sow, as well as those who go forth bearing
precious seed. That which they sow is something
very different from the word of the Kingdom, but it
has the same natural property of springing up ; and
the results of the mingled growth, strange and
baffling and melancholy as they are, are set forth
in this parable. Now we might take for granted that
the explanation would be unusually easy, because we
have not only our Lord's interpretation to fall back
upon, but also the analogy of the previous parable,
with which it has so much in common. This, however, is not the case. There is no parable of
which the popular apprehension is more thoroughly
blurred and useless. The outline is extremely
familiar, but hardly any attempt is made to connect
its teaching with the actual facts of religious
history or experience. The reason of this is not
far to seek. It is almost always assumed (assumed
even more than asserted) that this parable runs
on all fours with that of the drag net at the end
of the chapter. It is held to set forth the mixture of good and bad people in the visible Church,
and the hopelessness of any drastic attempt to
separate them until the day of judgment. This
reading of it is no doubt founded on a natural but
mistaken misapprehension of our Lord's interpretation.

But what is important to note just now is this, that it has passed into general and almost unquestioned acceptance entirely through the influence of the great Augustine. Commentators repeat one another from age to age with wonderful persistence, and no doubt they do wisely as a rule. But when we find out that St. Augustine himself adopted this interpretation under stress of controversy — of a controversy in which he was hard pressed for Scriptural arguments—we are not inclined to accept even his authority without looking into the matter. Everybody knows how eagerly texts and passages are pressed into the service of one side or the other when some burning question is agitating men's minds. Afterwards it is perceived that these texts and passages had not in fact any direct bearing upon the subject. Now St. Augustine and his friends were at strife especially with men like the Donatists, who were separating themselves from the general mass of Christians in order to find a greater purity of religious life and a stricter discipline. The parable of the drag-net obviously suited their side of the controversy. "If thou art a good fish in the Gospel net," cries the great Bishop to the Donatist, "what folly to try to get out again because there are bad fish in it too : possess thy soul in patience until the shore is reached : then shall they be cast away, but thou shalt be set apart for eternal life." Obviously, too, it was open to him to apply the parable of the tares in the same way. "If thou art good grain in the Master's field," he cries, "stay where thou art : do not mind the tares around thee : do not seek to root thyself up, and transplant thyself into some more select enclosure : *that* is not the Master's will : remain as thou art : grow where thou art : *no* good grain shall fail to be safely garnered when the great day of division comes." Now it may be fully allowed that St. Augustine was right — he had, at any rate, an immense deal to say for his position from Scripture. But it may be quite consistently denied that he had any right to impose this interpretation upon the parable of the tares. It is a common and an easy thing to press all manner of Scriptures into the service of some religious argument which is sound enough in itself; but the practice leads to any amount of confusion, and it is not really consistent with true reverence for the Scriptures themselves. Putting aside, therefore, St. Augustine's authority, as discredited by circumstances in this particular case, we perceive at once that the analogy of the former parable is altogether against his interpretation. "The good seed is the word of the Kingdom." That fundamental assumption ought surely to govern both parables of sowing. It ought surely to fix the meaning of the servants' question, "Didst thou not sow good seed in thy field?" If the good seed means sound Christian teaching, then by every rule of analogy the bad seed stands for such corrupt and spurious teachings as we know both from Scripture and from primitive Church history to have sprung up in extraordinary abundance wherever Christ was named. That presumption certainly holds the field until it is ruled out by some very convincing argument. Such an argument is found by many in our Lord's own words: "The good seed, these are the sons of the kingdom; and the tares are the sons of the evil one; and the enemy that sowed them is the devil." No doubt they would say, this is a very "hard saying," for it actually and without any reservation ascribes the origin and existence of unworthy Christians to the devil. Still it may be illustrated (though not exactly paralleled) from St. John viii. 44, where our Lord tells the unbelieving Jews that they are of their father the devil; from Acts xiii. 10, where St. Paul calls Elymas a son of the devil; and from I St. John iii. 10, where the Apostle seems to say that all those who do wickedness are children of the devil. Putting therefore this difficulty aside, we come back to the saying, "The good seed, these are the sons of the kingdom, and the tares are the sons of the evil one," and we compare it with what is said about the seed in the former parable. For brevity's sake we may content ourselves with the one last clause in the interpretation given by our Lord. Thus it runs:—St. Matthew xiii. 23, "He that was sown upon the good ground, this is he that heareth the word," etc.; St. Mark iv. 20, "Those are they that were sown upon the good ground, such as hear the word," etc.; St. Luke viii. 15, "That in the good ground, these are such as in an honest and good heart, having heard the word," etc. In all this variety one thing is perfectly clear. There is a deliberate confusion of language between the *seed* and the *people* in whose hearts the seed is sown. The

language which has been reported with so much
verbal difference and so much substantial agreement
by the Evangelists is as awkward in the Greek as
it is in English. If it were anywhere else we should
certainly say it was confusion of thought due to
careless and inaccurate mental processes. The seed
is one thing ; it is confessedly the word of the
Kingdom. The people who get sown with the seed,
who profit or do not profit by it, are another thing ;
they are confessedly the hearers of the word. But
of course there is no confusion of thought, and the
confusion of language so curiously palpable in the
record is intentional. Of set purpose our Lord
identified the seed and the products of the seed,
as embodied in the after life of the men who received it. Of set purpose, because a great truth
lies in that identification. It *is* profoundly true that
the word of the Kingdom grows into the man, so
that what he becomes is due not to himself, but
to it. The man himself becomes the product, the
embodiment, the realization, the fulfilment of the
Heavenly word. That is a truth which is readily
recognized as a very important one, and our Lord
sets it forth by this apparent confusion of ideas.
Here, as so often, He is willing to sacrifice effect—
that effect which is due to simple consistency of
imagery—to the need for setting forth the truth. It
is not possible to tell the story of the sower and
the seed very effectively, precisely because of this
confusion in our Lord's explanation. Those who
tell the story to children instinctively alter it so as
to avoid this awkward feature. That is a loss—a

loss which He deliberately incurred for a higher
gain. The religious life, He means to say, is not
merely human life touched and vivified by heavenly
influences. It is itself a thing come down from
Heaven; it is in fact the Life of Christ Himself
implanted in us, and in us asserting and displaying
its own divine characteristics. The "implanted
word" of St. James[1] (where he seems to be thinking of these parables of sowing) is identical with
the "Christ in us"[2] of St. Paul, Who does in a sense
supersede and supplant our own life.

Now, if we turn to the difficult saying about the
sons of the Kingdom and the sons of the evil one,
we see at once that our Lord spoke in perfect
keeping with the line which He had deliberately
adopted. He could not say anything else, since He
had already identified the seed sown with its living
products in human shape. The good seed is beyond
all question the word of the Cross; but it grows
into good Christians, and therefore it is "the sons
of the Kingdom." Similarly the evil seed, the tares,
is certainly false teaching; but it grows naturally
and necessarily into evil and degraded people, and
therefore "the tares are the sons of the evil one."
It will be seen that the expression which causes
so much difficulty—the tares are the children of the
evil one, and the enemy that sowed them is the
devil—is not really difficult at all if we recognize
the fact that it is an extremely compressed statement
which sets forth with startling brevity the result of
a long process. In their beginning the tares are

---

[1] James i. 21.   [2] Gal. ii. 20.

false teachings, specially designed to counteract the good effects of the word of God. In their end, by virtue of that identification to which attention has been called above, they are bad people—people such as St. John speaks of as children of the devil.[1] Neither the sons of the Kingdom nor the sons of the evil one are planted ready-made in the field. To entertain any such notion is to throw into utter confusion, not Christian theology only, but also all the imagery, and (so to speak) machinery of these parables of sowing. What is sown is merely seed ; but the seed grows up and bears fruit after its kind ; and since this fruit is human conduct and character, the seed becomes identified with the men into whose lives it has grown.

This reading of the parable is really forced upon us by the analogy of its companion picture ; it is also indicated by our Lord Himself. "The Son of man," He says, "shall send forth His angels, and they shall gather out of His Kingdom *all things that cause stumbling*, and them that do iniquity." What has to be removed is twofold, first *things*, then *persons*, corresponding exactly to the tares in their early and in their developed state ; beginning as pernicious teachings, ending as evildoers. It is, of course, in perfect keeping with our Lord's methods of speech that both things and persons are cast into the furnace of fire. The "beast" and the "false prophet" (who represent, presumably, not individuals but systems of violence and error) are to be "cast alive into the lake of fire burning with brimstone."[2]

[1] 1 John iii. 10.   [2] Rev. xix 20.

Again, this reading of the parable gives a wonderfully vivid portraiture of the Kingdom from a point of view which is beyond question important and true. Nothing is more certain, although it could hardly have been anticipated, than that the good seed never has the field to itself, and did not from the first. There are rival teachings, industriously spread, eagerly accepted by many, fit to deceive the very elect, which have their proper outcome in a luxuriant crop of corrupt and unsanctified lives. Whatever objection may be taken to this position (and this objection will not be ignored) it is certain that it is in perfect concord with the later books of the New Testament, and with early Christian opinion. St. Paul lets us know that his steps were dogged all over the world by Judaizers, who were evidently stirred up to a sort of frenzy of proselytizing zeal by their hatred of the free grace which he preached. What he felt about them and their converts may be gathered from such a passage as this, " Beware of the dogs, beware of the evil workers, beware of the concision "[1]— a term of angry contempt, this last, for those who called themselves " the circumcision." Or from his passionate exclamation : " I would that they which unsettle you would even cut themselves off "[2] (perhaps "mutilate themselves"). St. Paul would have heartily agreed that both the authors and the victims of these Judaizing teachings were sons of the evil one. So would St. John of those who embraced the errors against which he testifies in his epistles. " If any man cometh unto you and

---

[1] Phil. iii. 2.   [2] Gal. v. 12.

bringeth not this [true] teaching, receive him not
into your house and give him no greeting; for he
that giveth him greeting partaketh in his evil
works."[1] It would appear that the false teachings
which he denounces in his Epistles, were those
"docetic" doctrines which afterwards became so
popular, and gave rise to a considerable literature,
nominally Christian. Their common ground was
that Christ did not really suffer, because suffering and
humiliation are unworthy of a Divine Being, and
impossible. He did but cheat the wicked Jews by
seeming to suffer until His hour of victory was come.
His humanity, in fact, was illusory. It is difficult
for us to understand how this kind of teaching could
appeal to anyone, for it runs dead counter to the
deepest convictions of all men now, whether believers
or unbelievers. But we can readily see that in the
days when it was popular it was tares, pure and
simple. Such a teaching, so far as it grew into anything at all, could only grow into children of the
evil one—into men and women of no earnestness,
no love of truth, no sense of duty, no moral restraint,
no spiritual enthusiasm.

Still more emphatic is the same apostle's testimony
in the Epistles to the Seven Churches in Asia. In
the teaching of the Nicolaitans, and of "the woman
Jezebel which calleth herself a prophetess," we have
apparently in a rudimentary form the spurious
Christianity which afterwards developed into Gnosticism, or, at any rate, into its coarser forms. It was
their boast that to them it was given to know "the

[1] 2 John 10, 11.

deep things of Satan "[1]—a horrible parody upon "the deep things of God" of which St. Paul had spoken. To know all things, to gauge them by experiment, and so to master and appropriate them—irrespective of moral distinctions—was the great end proposed to themselves by these people; it was their notion of the way of life.   Their doctrine must have been professedly Christian, and had considerable following in Christian communities like Pergamum and Thyatira. No doubt it represented the extreme revolt from the strictness of Judaism, disguised itself in a show of spirituality, and sheltered itself under the name of St. Paul.   No doubt this seed also had its successes and its failures, but it found plenty of fertile soil awaiting it.   We should hardly be wrong in supposing that in the second century there were as many Gnostics as Christians.   If they failed to continue, the failure was not due to any lack of numbers or of popularity, but to the absence of moral earnestness, which was an integral part of their system.   They did not die for the Christian faith they were supposed to hold.   Why should they?   Why should they not deny Christ, and offer sacrifice to idols, if necessity arose?   They *knew* better, of course, and knowing is everything.   What a man *did* with his hands, or any other part of him, could not affect the mind, which is immaterial and free.   The perfect Gnostic regarded all actions as indifferent in themselves, and therefore took the line which at the moment was easiest and pleasantest.   But this very adaptability, this lack of what all men count as "principle," was their destruc-

[1] Rev. ii. 24.

tion. Those who cannot die cannot live either—in the long run. The Christians lived on, though constantly thinned out by persecution, because the tremendous earnestness of their convictions made their mutual coherence perfect, and filled them with missionary ardour. The Gnostics came to an end because they had no very strong reason for being Gnostics—or anything else—if it turned out to be inconvenient. So the Lord of the harvest sent forth His angels (in disguise), and they gathered out of His kingdom these stumbling-blocks of Gnosticism and these pseudo - Christians who had no moral earnestness.

In this connection we may look that objection in the face to which we referred above. We all feel secretly uneasy at the extreme vehemence with which false teachers are denounced in the New Testament. We think of the many forms of professedly Christian teaching *now* which we consider (may be) extremely erroneous and pernicious, and we wonder whether our Lord would have said that He "hated" them; whether St. John would have had us refuse to their teachers the ordinary civilities of social life ; whether he himself would have rushed out of a public bath when one of them entered. If we allow ourselves to think of acting like this towards any religious leader of the present day, we perceive at once that it would not only be unmannerly, it would be bigoted and unchristian. And yet it is not easy to say clearly where the difference comes in. We might say that such action would be incongruous and open to reproach *now*, because the strength and heat of

Christian conviction has confessedly cooled down ; the faith is not *everything* to us as it was to them. But then no increase of conviction or of earnestness would make such action any more possible to us. Dismissing all reasons founded upon indifference, or upon a toleration which is not Christian, is it not true that we have learnt from experience to draw a deep and wide distinction between faith and morals, creed and character ? The man who differs from us *toto cœlo* in religion may be as good as we—perhaps better. "There's good and bad in all religions," is the popular verdict, and it is largely justified by the facts, as far as we may know them. We must acknowledge that frankly, and it absolutely prohibits any hatred or lack of kindness towards those that preach "another gospel," however much we may dislike it. But we must as frankly acknowledge that the point of view in the New Testament is quite different. The heresies denounced there are always immoral. They have a likeness to Christianity on the doctrinal side, but no sympathy with the sternness of its moral teaching. The Cross has always been taken out in order to please men, in order to get rid of the hard necessity for crucifying sin and self. The very strong things said of false teachers by the sacred writers can only be applied to such as destroy the moral power of Christianity and make the word of the Cross of none effect. The tares which are destined to be burnt are not merely theologically wrong : they are morally corrupt.

It may of course be asked why our Lord should so pointedly have ignored the distinction between religious faith and moral conduct which has since become so clear; why He should have assumed that they were practically identical, and allowed His immediate followers to assume it too. No sufficient answer is forthcoming yet, but it may go some way if we point out that our Lord often speaks in a way which is extraordinarily abbreviated and compressed. He speaks of things absolutely, as though here and now, which are yet only foreseen in their essential tendencies, in their certain (though remote) results. From His point of view, it may be, falsity in faith and failure in character are identical, because in the ultimate truth and outcome of things they must be. Amidst the infinite confusions and cross-purposes of the world (especially in its present complexity) faith and morals seem to have little connection. In the end—or rather we should say at bottom—they are the same. All conduct is governed by motives; the only sufficient motives are furnished "by the faith of the Son of God, who loved me and gave Himself for me."[1] To tamper with that faith is to impair those motives; to impair those motives is to wreck the character which is determined by them. It is possible to acknowledge the truth of this without ignoring any of the facts of modern life.

Probably it is in the Mission Field that we should expect to find the best illustrations of this parable as of the preceding. We may take the case, *e.g.*, of the Maoris of New Zealand, a singularly intelligent race of savages who were converted to

[1] Gal. ii. 20.

Christianity with unusual ease and completeness. Nevertheless, the greater part of them relapsed into a horrid fanaticism made up out of discordant elements of Old Testament and New Testament teaching, mingled with sheer delusion and imposture, and totally without moral power. Or we may take an individual example, very instructive in its way, from the brief history of Zulu Christianity. This man was the most promising pupil of one of the mission establishments in Natal. Very well educated, very industrious, and very capable, he has reached a position which few, if any, of his countrymen can boast of. He remains also a religious man, to all appearance. But he is a polygamist. He took a second wife on the plea that his first had no children. He took a third for no reason at all except that she was young and good-looking. These things he did, not like many who relapse into heathenism, but as a religious man, basing his conduct upon the examples of Abraham, David, and other Old Testament saints. It is not necessary to judge him too harshly. Part of the blame rests upon those Christian teachers who put the Bible into the hands of savages as the word of God, and do not explain to them that the ethics of the Old Testament are rudimentary, imperfect, and therefore obsolete, because accommodated to the hardness of men's hearts and the needs of an age which has long ago been left behind in the moral education of mankind. But when we consider that polygamy is the greatest of all hindrances to the spread of the Gospel in those regions, and when we perceive

how great is the influence of this man's example
for evil, then we must acknowledge that here is a
definite and veritable example of the tares which
are so industriously sown upon the top of the good
seed. Because this man's actual life, before the eyes
of his people, is the product of the false doctrine he
has imbibed, he is (in our Lord's language) a son
of the evil one, and the enemy that sowed him is
the devil. Lest we should esteem ourselves as being
beyond the reach of such sowing, we may recall
the fact that Mormonism drew countless "converts"
from the Protestant populations of north - west
Europe. If Mormonism is dead, or dying, to-day,
that is not because religious influences have been
too much for it, but solely because political circumstances led to its being suppressed (practically) by
force of arms. Indeed it is not possible to shut
one's eyes to the fact that a tendency to Antinomianism—to a throwing over of the moral law—
constantly besets spiritual Christianity. The belated
legalism which practically confounds the two dispen-
sations, which regards Calvary itself as a new and
superior Sinai, which (in the teeth of St. Paul's
Epistles) persists in treating Christianity as a mass
of rules and observances, is such a hateful thing
that it provokes men to rush into the opposite and
even worse error. The eternal preaching against
"good works" which was fashionable fifty years
ago is past and gone, thank God. It was tares.
So far as it had any effect, it killed out Christian
earnestness and stifled the voice of the Spirit in
innumerable hearts. "Follow Me," said Christ, "and

thou shalt have treasure in heaven." " Do not follow Him," cried the fashionable preacher in effect ; " if you do, you will be doing good works, and then you will not be saved by grace." There is a very real danger about Christian activity. But to kill the activity in order to avoid the danger is a travesty of St. Paul's teaching, and is so remote from our Lord's teaching as not even to be a travesty of it. There is then a constant tendency in Christian teaching, under the influence of human impatience and exaggeration, to deteriorate into something which has no moral power. We cannot forget, when we take note of this fact, that the peasants of Palestine seem to have been convinced that *the wheat itself degenerated into tares.* Apparently that is impossible. What looks like degeneration is really (in either case) the insidious and inexplicable substitution of something quite different. The moral failures of Christianity are not due in any case to any inferiority or unsuitability in the good seed, the word of the Kingdom. The field hath tares, because an enemy hath sown them.

It is now open to us to indicate exactly where the " moral " of the parable comes in. The tares were not to be pulled up lest the growing wheat, whose roots were intertwined with those of the tares, should be rooted up too. False doctrines are *not* to be violently suppressed. The wish to do so is sure to arise, because the damage which they cause is very serious and very lamentable. The kind of toleration which regards them with indifference has no place whatever in the New Testament.

E

If there be any methods of discouraging the tares
without violence, let them be used by all means;
but pulling them up is mischievous and forbidden.
It is bound to do more harm than good. No saying
of our Lord's has been more clearly illustrated in
the history of the Church than this. The doctrines,
for instance, of the Priscillianists were tares without
doubt, like all the Manichæan teachings which in
so many forms, and with such a strange persistency,
invaded the Christian ground. But when, in the
year 385, Bishop Priscillian and six of his followers
were put to death by a Christian ruler at the
instigation of Christian prelates, not only was a
dreadful wrong done to these unhappy people, but a
frightful injury was inflicted upon the more unhappy
Church of Christ. No doubt the tares were somewhat thinned by this violence, but the harm done
to the true grain was incalculable. Much of the best
teaching of Christianity withered away when persecution of Christians by Christians was begun. Still
more noteworthy is the case of the Albigenses in
the twelfth and thirteenth centuries. Their teachings
also were tares, pure and simple. The assertion that
they were a sect of an evangelical or Protestant
character is absolutely false. They too were Manichæan, believed in two Gods, held matrimony to be
sinful, and encouraged suicide. Whatever earnestness
of conviction or severity of life there may have been
among them, it is clear that the whole drift and
tendency of their doctrines was immoral. Simon
de Montfort and other leaders of the crusade against
them may be credited with a sincere detestation of

the mischievous propaganda which they carried on among the ignorant populations of Southern France. But the methods and results of the crusade were equally horrible. In the most literal way the wheat was rooted up with the tares. Albigenses and Catholics were slain without distinction, and it was left to God to "know His own." If from individuals we turn to doctrines, we see at once that along with the errors of the Manichæans (bad enough no doubt) there perished out of the land all the finer feelings, all the gentler and kindlier counsels, which belong to the religion of Christ. The damage to the wheat was simply incalculable. It is not possible to use any violence, even of language, towards false doctrines in the field of Christ without doing some harm to the choice and tender growths of which He Himself is the patron. And the spoiling of these is a terrible price to have to pay for the partial destruction of the very worst tares.

IV.

THE PARABLE OF THE MUSTARD SEED

St. Matt. xiii. 31–32.

Another parable put he forth unto them, saying, The kingdom of heaven is like to a grain of mustard seed, which a man took, and sowed in his field:

Which indeed is the least of all seeds: but when it is grown, it is the greatest among herbs, and becometh a tree, so that the birds of the air come and lodge in the branches thereof.

St. Mark iv. 30–32.

And he said, Whereunto shall we liken the kingdom of God? or with what comparison shall we compare it?

It is like a grain of mustard seed, which, when it is sown in the earth, is less than all the seeds that be in the earth:

But when it is sown, it groweth up, and becometh greater than all herbs, and shooteth out great branches; so that the fowls of the air may lodge under the shadow of it.

St. Luke xiii. 18, 19.

Then said he, Unto what is the kingdom of God like? and whereunto shall I resemble it?

It is like a grain of mustard seed, which a man took, and cast into his garden; and it grew, and waxed a great tree; and the fowls of the air lodged in the branches of it.

WE may safely assume that this parable and that of the leaven are closely connected, without being at all identical in meaning. That seems to follow from the way in which they lie together in the Gospels, especially in that of St. Luke, where they appear isolated from the others, and in an entirely different connection. They are obviously alike in this, that they both mean extension, growth, development—and that, rapid and surprising. But they differ as obviously in this, that in the one case the extension takes an outward and visible form, and is embodied in a concrete shape; whereas in the other case the extension is that of a powerful agent working invisibly to the human eye, but producing a very great effect upon the whole mass with which it has to do. It is the same activity that is really at work in both cases—the activity of what we call vegetable life—but the two forms in which it manifests itself so surprisingly are somewhat sharply contrasted: they are complemental the one to the other.

Now if we bring to the elucidation of these parables the same historical tests which we have already found so useful, they will stand out before our eyes with the utmost distinctness both in their likeness and their unlikeness. After the initial stage in which the word of the Kingdom is first disseminated, and after the ensuing period of false teaching and of moral perversion, the next clearly marked stage is that of rapid growth. Nothing is more astonishing than the quickness with which the Christian faith spread, and the Christian Society ramified, throughout the Roman Empire during the centuries of persecution, after the first great crop of Gnostic and kindred heresies had begun to die down. The persecution itself did not stimulate the growth of Christianity: that is a blunder founded on certain rhetorical expressions of the early Christian writers.

The indirect evidence is overwhelming that, whilst the *quality* of the Christian converts was improved, their *quantity* was largely diminished by the terror of the State. But the persecution was itself to a great degree dependent upon the rapid spread of the new religion. The rulers of this world were frightened by the wholesale proselytism that they saw going on. With that curious mixture of timidity and obstinacy which so often afflicts the mere politician, they apprehended all manner of dreadful consequences from the growth of the Church, and persisted in thinking that they could stop it. Anyhow, that growth is *the* great fact of these centuries. The words of Tertullian addressed to the Emperor about the year 200 A.D. are no doubt rhetorical (like all his words), but still substantially true. "We are a people of yesterday, and yet we have filled every place belonging to you —cities, islands, castles, towns, assemblies, your very camp, your tribes and companies, your palace, senate, forum. We leave you your temples only. We can count your armies ; *our* numbers in a single province will be greater." Never was boast more unwisely made, but never was it more justified by the facts. It was the mysterious power of growth in the insignificant mustard-seed, which no man may explain. It was the equally mysterious capacity of the unseen leaven to impart its own state to the kindred matter surrounding it. This power, this capacity, was and is inherent in the new religion itself. That the sudden growth of those centuries was greatly favoured by circumstances need not be doubted. Neither should it be denied that under certain other circumstances the extension of the Kingdom has been greatly checked and even brought to a standstill. All the same, it has asserted itself so often and so remarkably that we are obliged to recognize it, on the ground of history and experience alone, as an inherent property of Christianity. It does not belong to us to prophesy, but we may take note of the signs of the times, and these signs all point to another approaching epoch of rapid expansion in India, in China, in Africa. As long as the word of the Kingdom is really the word of the Cross, it does not seem to be sterilized (much as it is hindered) either by divisions or by corruptions. The minority of men, who have "honest and good" hearts, still receive it with joy; and the majority, who do not really appreciate it, will nevertheless acquiesce in it after a season. History, therefore, and experience bear witness in the very clearest manner to this particular aspect of the Kingdom, so picturesquely put before us in this pair of parables.

These two methods of extension, however, are not only to be treated as two forms of the same activity: they fall to be considered in their contrast. The one is the growth of the Christian Society, the other is the spread of Christian ideas—of the Christian spirit, as it is sometimes expressed. These are so far from being identical, or even coincident, that where there is most extension one way there may be least the other way. And again very few people are equally capable of appreciating both. It may even be said of most that they "hold to the one and despise the other"—a phenomenon to which we shall have to return. The mustard - seed comes first — not necessarily because it represents a more fundamental or necessary aspect of things. It was in our Lord's time a recognized symbol of something almost too tiny to be seen, or at least to be worth taking into account. " If ye have faith *as a grain of mustard-seed*," He said, indicating the least imaginable quantity, so as the quality was good. But the mustard-seed, tiny as it is, grows up into a *tree*. Not, of course, a forest tree, like an oak or an elm, but something which may fairly be called a tree in comparison with the plants and bushes and shrubs of the garden in which it was sown. Perhaps the birds are the best judges of what is, and what is not, a tree ; and they decide the question in favour of the mustard by finding its branches stout enough and leafy enough to roost in. Now this thing which towers above its neighbours in the garden, and rises to the dignity and uses of a tree, is just the tiny seed developed and grown to its full size and shape according to the law of life which was in the seed. There is an absolute continuity of life—vegetable life —between mustard seed and mustard tree. It has not increased by mere mechanical or arithmetical addition. It has absorbed all this, by which it has grown, into itself from air or soil, has incorporated it all with itself, retaining all the time its own oneness and identity. In a word the mustard tree is *a body :* not, of course, an animal body like ours, but still a body with an organized life of its own. However inferior the vegetable world may be accounted, the tree still presents the one essential feature of a structural variety in unity, the whole frame being permeated by the mysterious principle which we call life. Downwards to the furthest fibres of its roots, and upwards to the highest twigs of its branches, the tree through all its various and ever-varying parts is one, and is (in a true though limited sense) alive. There we have the essential truth of a "body," and there we come into touch with all that teaching of St. Paul about the Church as a "body" with which we are so familiar.

Just now, however, we must go back to the parable of the mustard tree in order to observe that in it our Lord distinctly regarded the Kingdom of Heaven as a visible and corporate institution, as a religious body among others which it was to overtop and overshadow, in a word as the Christian Church. That is only *one* aspect of the Kingdom, one amongst many, one which is immediately supplemented by a cognate but different aspect: but still it *is* one aspect of the Kingdom. There would not be any sense in the parable if there were not to be a visible Society whose rapid and unexpected growth should make it conspicuous in the eyes of all men. Christian history emphatically assures us that there was such a Society. Ask every heathen emperor of the first three centuries; ask every heathen writer who deigns to mention the Christians: what they saw with fear and aversion, what they waged war with to the death, was not an opinion, or a cult, or a set of principles, but a Society which held all together, which had its officers and its passwords, which threatened the security of the State, just because it was coherent and corporate, which seemed to them (who knew not the distinction between civil and religious) an *imperium in imperio.* When we speak of the Christian Church as "ramifying" throughout the Empire, we use the word quite accurately. To "ramify" is to throw out branches, like the trees above us; or still more like certain lowly plants which drive their multitudinous stems under or along the surface of the ground, and send up continual shoots in every place. Such was the spread of the Church. Everywhere she had her branches, her members, her congregations; and everywhere they were one, not disconnected, not isolated, not separate. It was precisely because they divined this fact that the rulers fell into that kind of panic which more than anything else leads to blind fury and cruelty. It was not an epidemic of Christian opinion with which they had to deal, but the endless ramifications of a corporate Society which would presently supersede the State. No doubt they misunderstood the nature and object of the unity. We know that it was essentially a unity of the Spirit; but we are bound to acknowledge that it was expressed and fortified by a corresponding unity of outward religious life. The "one Lord, one faith, one baptism" was represented and reinforced by the Christians being "all partakers of that one bread." Without venturing on disputed ground, we may add that a loose but effectual organization served the purposes of inter-communication, of mutual support and edification, of necessary discipline. Whatever else, then, Christianity was to them that

were without, it was in the first place a *Society*
which grew at a surprising rate, and yet remained
unmistakably one. Whatever else it was to them
that were within, it was unquestionably a *Society*,
a Society for holy living and mutual help, a Society
which Christ Himself had taught them to call His
Church, a Society of which St. Paul had written
things so high and glorious as to pass man's understanding. A heathen and a Christian in the fifth
century (let us say) after Christ would have found
this parable equally clear and equally remarkable.
"As for the other parables," the heathen would
have said, "I know not what they mean, but this
one is plain enough. Your mustard tree has indeed
grown prodigiously, as your Master said. If one
had not known, one would not have believed that
it had continuously expanded from the tiny seed
sown in Judæa, and yet remained identical with
it. It has filled the world with its branches, and
yet it is essentially one."

Now if these things cannot be gainsaid, if the
Kingdom of Heaven was originally revealed (in
one aspect of it) as a corporate body endowed with
a marvellous capacity of growth, if St. Paul urged
and illustrated and enforced this corporate aspect of
the Kingdom with the greatest earnestness, then it is
certain that no loyal Christian can fail to hold a doctrine of "the Church" and to regard it as a doctrine
immensely important. What is so profoundly to
be regretted is not so much that Christians have
no fixed and common doctrine of the Church, as
that a multitude of them have no doctrine at all.

They will not hear of it. The very sound affronts them because they vaguely connect it with some ecclesiastical despotism, or some unfounded pretensions to authority. They will hear of Christianity as a set of opinions, as a rule of good living, as a divine influence, but the corporate aspect of the Church does not appeal to them at all; it only angers them. There *must* be something very wrong in this, because this very aspect is distinctly intimated by our Lord, emphatically dwelt upon by St. Paul, and most prominently presented in history. Loyalty and honesty alike demand that we should face the question of "the Church." It is not enough to admit that Christianity spread through the world like leaven. It also grew like a tree—like *a* seed (our Lord says) which grew into *a* tree, very unexpectedly big, but still *a* tree, not a grove of trees, not even a group of trees. The Christianity which overcame the world by suffering and persisting, was emphatically the Christianity of one Church, which had, no doubt, its internal troubles, but never permitted anyone to doubt its organic unity. It is impossible in this connection not to refer to the teaching of St. Paul, according to which this Church (the mustard tree of the parable) is at once the Body and the Bride of Christ—nay, in a sense His *alter ego* —which can hardly be discriminated from Himself. "As the body is one" (he says) "and hath many members, and all the members of the body, being many, are one body; so also is Christ"[1]—by which, of course, he means the Church of Christ. It is the simple old

[1] 1 Cor. xii. 12.

lesson of organic unity combined with an endless variety of function which was urged by Menenius Agrippa long before St. Paul's time upon the warring members of the Roman commonwealth. Christians, like members of any other body corporate, have duties towards one another and have need one of another. "So also is the Church," St. Paul meant. But he did not write that. Something came into his mind which made him substitute at the last moment another name, and he actually wrote "so also is *Christ.*" Now that is an extraordinary change. In another man it could only be put down to an unaccountable confusion of thought—or possibly to one of those brilliant intuitions by which a magnificent truth is compressed into a single unexpected word. In St. Paul it is something more than a brilliant intuition. The Church and Christ are so far *one* that in a passage like this—which is not rhetorical but didactic, and concerned with practical duties—the name of Christ may be substituted for the name of the Church. In other words, "Christ" may be written where "the Church" is unquestionably meant. For no one doubts that it is the Church in a corporate capacity which resembles the human body with all its members, organs, and functions, bound together in a living unity. What is the justification for this? What is the justification for that bracketing together (if I may so express it) of Christ and the Church in Eph. iii. 21 (R.V.), "Unto Him be the glory in the Church and in Christ Jesus unto all generations for ever and ever"? Only one thing could justify such language, and that is St. Paul's

doctrine of the mystical oneness of Christ and His
Church, by virtue of which she is His body, His
bride, His other self, the recipient and reflexion of
the sum total of His glories and His attributes.
If this sounds exaggerated, let us call before us that
word "fulness" (πλήρωμα) which the Apostle uses so
pointedly in his letters to the sister churches of
Ephesus and Colossæ. "It was the good pleasure
of the Father," he writes, "that in Him [Christ]
should *all the fulness* dwell."[1]   Accordingly, "in
Him dwelleth *all the fulness* of the Godhead
bodily."[2]   "The fulness," used of a person, certainly
means the sum total of attributes and glories. These
dwelt in Christ "bodily," *i.e.*, according to the nature
of the Incarnation, whereby He was "found in
fashion as a man." But this is not all. This same
"fulness," which is Christ's, is realized in the Church.[3]
She *is* His fulness. There is not anything divine
and heavenly in our Lord which is not found in the
Church. Nor is this all. In Eph. v. we have a
well-known passage which is rhetorical certainly,
but none the less true in its way. Christ and His
Church are compared to the ideal married pair,
the husband and wife of Gen. ii., and the relation
between them is declared to be the same. "This
mystery is great," he says, "but I speak in regard of
Christ and of the Church." The "mystery" to which
he refers is the fact that by the will of God husband
and wife become one flesh, so that as our Lord says
"They are no more twain, but one flesh."[4]

---

[1] Col. i. 19.   [2] Col. ii. 9.
[3] Eph. i. 23.   [4] Matt. xix. 6.

Now no reverent person will dismiss these things as figures of speech, or flights of rhetoric; nor will he be content to accept them in a merely negative way without trying to take them into his actual faith. No one who wants to be in harmony with the teaching of the New Testament can possibly be satisfied with mere "individualism" or mere "congregationalism" in religion. The inclination to do this is extremely widespread, because the temptation to do so is very strong. Amidst our present divisions it is infinitely more convenient to be content with personal religion and to have *no* doctrine of "the Church," to ignore the Church, to treat all "Church" matters as though they belonged exclusively to the realm of personal preference, or of local convenience, or of chance. Almost all Christians who glory in "undenominational" religion, and many others beside, have practically *no* doctrine of the Church. They have much to say about "Churches," as if polygamy were the original law of Heaven; but if they ever speak of "the Church," they only mean the arithmetical aggregate of such Christians as have (in their opinion) obtained like precious faith with themselves. Such a low and poor conception could never have inspired the glowing language of the Apostle. If the Church is only the numerical sum-total of all those who are Christians, then a considerable part of the New Testament is exaggerated and misleading. The Church which is the Bride, the Lamb's wife, is not a multitude of individuals, nor is it an aggregation or a federation of religious bodies. No one could ever believe that, unless he felt himself shut up to it by the cruel exigency of a poor and stunted creed, and therefore forced himself to accept it. No doubt "the Church" is in one sense made up of congregations (which are also called "Churches"), just as these are made up of individuals; but it is a great deal more. In that vision of things eternal which was given to St. Paul, the Church appears as the counterpart of Christ Himself, existing from the beginning, created for Him (as Eve was for Adam) to be His spouse, His other self, the recipient and reflexion of His perfections. That is of course an *ideal*, and ideals are notoriously hard to deal with and easy to deride. To this day it is evident that the ideal has not been realized within our ken, except in the most imperfect and fragmentary way. But it is not *man's* ideal; it is God's ideal, with which He started (if it is permitted to say so), fore-knowing the end from the beginning, foreseeing the perfect and the final in the partial and temporary, and loving it as His own worthy of Himself. In a mystical sense, but in a sense not the less real and true, the Church existed before ever there was a single Christian in the world. The Bride was foreknown and foreordained and called and justified and glorified from all eternity in and with and for the Bridegroom. So then it is in the highest sense true that we individual Christians do not make the Church (that is only an earthly way of putting it); it is rather the Church that makes us, as one by one, in time and place, we are "added unto the Church," and are made to share her eternal glories which are Christ's. If we should agree that some such teaching is demanded of us, if we would give any serious heed to the things which are said about the Church in the New Testament—if this be the true vision of the Bride, the Lamb's wife—the question instantly arises, "How does this doctrine of the ideal Church stand related to, stand connected with, the actual and visible organization of the Christian Society upon earth?" To which question, inevitable though it be, no satisfactory answer has ever been given. But, nevertheless, two principles may be laid down which will command general assent — principles which *must* govern any answer that shall be found. First, it is impossible to *identify* the ideal Church of the New Testament writings with any hierarchy, or with any ecclesiastical organization upon earth. And this, not only because the ideal Church includes the faithful departed as well as the living, but also because *even as far as this world alone is concerned* the visible Church has been and is, in a multitude of ways, a most grievous misrepresentation of the heavenly Spouse of Christ. It is easy to understand the charm, the overmastering attraction of the Church of Rome, from certain obvious points of view. Above all she stands pronouncedly for that unity which is itself so pronounced a feature in the New Testament presentation of the true religion. But even a limited acquaintance with history tells us beyond the possibility of doubt that this Church (which is, and must be, "always the same") has been a really hideous caricature of the true Bride. It has been the

F

veritable home and haunt of deliberate deceits, of boundless ambitions, of merciless cruelty, of ravening covetousness, of every sinful passion which is most contrary to the Spirit of Christ. If it has to a great extent laid aside the exercise of these, it is perfectly evident that it has only done so because the course of this world has forced such abnegation upon it. Moreover, while it is true that the Roman Church has purged itself of the worst features of the past, it is also true that—taken the whole world over—it presents the strangest mixture of what is noble and beautiful with what is contemptible and revolting, all claiming the same "infallible" foundation. Again, if it is impossible to identify the Bride of Christ in any close way with the Church of Rome, neither will anything else satisfy us which it is possible to define as "the Church." All such definitions are clearly more or less arbitrary and exclusive on the one hand (for even the test of baptism shuts out many "naturally Christian souls" whom we must claim for Christ), and on the other hand they are too vague and inclusive morally. But, secondly, it is equally impossible to assert that there is *no* connection between the ideal Church and the organized Society of believers. St. Paul addressed that Society, as it existed in his day, as the body of Christ. He always had it more or less in view when he spoke about the Church. He had apparently no inkling whatever of that theory of the "invisible" Church which finds so much favour to-day as a convenient method of escape from a great difficulty. That there are in fact a certain number of souls at any given moment which are in a state of grace, and destined to remain so, is a statement difficult to deny, and it is easy to add that *these* form the true Church of Christ at that moment. But the New Testament has no such teaching, and St. Paul's way of speaking to the Corinthians and others is certainly not based upon it. He writes to them all as Christians, and speaks of them collectively as the body of Christ. Thus we are obliged to believe that there is a real relationship between the ideal Church in Scripture and the actual Church in history; and yet we are obliged to believe that the relationship is not one of identity, nor yet of close correspondence. Apparently it cannot be ascertained what the relationship is, and yet our faith will be imperfect and our conduct ill-guided if we do not acknowledge the relationship. The glory and the loveliness of the Bride was meant to shed its lustre upon the poorest state of things in the Church below, and to add dignity and romance to its lowliest duties. Everywhere and in all things Christian people were to read the unearthly vision of the Bride into the most prosaic and even unpleasant features of their "Church" life on earth. That involves a great and trying difficulty, which can neither be solved by hasty assertions and assumptions on the one hand, nor by evasions and denials on the other.

One thing is clear. It is easy to understand how Christian people can take the most opposite views of the questions which divide them. But it is impossible to understand how they can fail to grieve over those divisions themselves; still more how they can find pleasure in them. They stand in the most glaring opposition to the Divine Ideal. They have gone far to efface, and that with something like cynical effrontery, one of the chief features in that ideal. The one Bride of the second Adam, the Mother of all living souls, is resolved into—what one cannot bring oneself to write. This is not a question of ecclesiastical opinion: it is a question of believing the Scripture or not. In the whole Bible there is, as a fact, no *hint* that the Church was ever to be other than *one*, closely and intimately *one*, whether in its ideal or in its actual state.

It remains, therefore, to see in this parable a picture of growth, rapid, unexpected, from extremely small and unpromising beginnings to surprising greatness; and this too the growth of a living and organized body, having its own proper vitality, and remaining essentially one and the same through all its processes of development and of differentiation. That is the one plain and certain lesson which Christian history abundantly confirms and illustrates. It is permissible to point out that Christian history does at least *suggest* a further meaning in those words, "so that the birds of the heaven come and lodge in the branches thereof." That saying may, of course, be merely a picturesque touch intended to emphasize the unexpected size to which the tree has grown. Birds do not perch upon anything weak and insecure. But it is easy to find in it more than that. These birds have played a part in a former parable, that of the good seed, and there they were interpreted as messengers of the evil one. Idle thoughts, wandering desires, undisciplined imaginations, the infinite preoccupations of secular life, snatch away the seed sown in the heart. Vary this imagery a little, and we see in the birds that come to lodge in the branches of the mustard-seed a lively picture of that multitude of incongruous things which have established themselves under the shadow of the visible Church. Nothing has, in fact, been more remarkable. There is hardly any kind of taste, of pursuit, however alien to the meaning and purport of Christianity, which has not flourished under the patronage of the Church, or at least availed itself of its resources. The pleasant pictures which Isaiah denounced (ii. 16), and all the costly luxuries reprobated in Rev. xviii., have found their chosen home in Church establishments. The stern iconoclasm of primitive Christianity has given place to the passionate cultivation of art for art's sake. Even such things as alchemy, astrology, and magic, things plainly repugnant to Christian piety, have been eagerly pursued by Churchmen, and in the Cloister. All this has been the inevitable result of the greatness of the visible Church. Whatsoever was " in the air " and " on the wing " has been irresistibly attracted to the Church, and sooner or later has found a lodgment beneath her spreading arms. It may be that our Lord intended to intimate this. Anyhow it is true.

V.

THE PARABLE OF THE LEAVEN

St. Matt. xiii. 33.

Another parable spake he unto them; The kingdom of heaven is like unto leaven, which a woman took, and hid in three measures of meal, till the whole was leavened.

St. Luke xiii. 20, 21.

And again he said, Whereunto shall I liken the kingdom of God?

It is like leaven, which a woman took and hid in three measures of meal, till the whole was leavened.

THE more we dwell upon the Kingdom of Heaven as an outward and visible growth— the growth of an organized Society which in fact rapidly overshadowed all the other religious bodies in its neighbourhood — the more we are bound to balance this presentation of the Kingdom by the one which immediately follows. It is a sore evil in religious thought that it is so generally unbalanced, and nowhere is the evil more rampant than here. For a vast number of people the greatness and the oneness of the visible Church are everything. This aspect of the Kingdom fills their whole field of vision, and they have no eyes for any other. And so a partial and one-sided apprehension of truth lays them open to miserable servitude to error. On the other hand there are multitudes who have seen so clearly that the visible Church is not everything, that they refuse to believe that it concerns them at all; whereby they give the lie to Scripture and our Lord, and disable themselves from laying hold upon one whole side of the faith. Most helpful is it, therefore, to take note how these two parables of the mustard-seed and the leaven mutually supplement and complement one another, closely connected and yet sharply contrasted. Each is a parable of growth, and of growth due to the action of a living force, but of growth so different as to have apparently nothing else in common. The leaven works secretly, it works from within, it works pervasively, it works not by an access of size, but by the spread of an altered condition. The Kingdom is a Church: it is also (and as truly) an influence, a moral, religious, and spiritual influence, permeating society and penetrating far beyond the limits of any ecclesiastical organization. What our Lord meant by "leavened" seems to have been much the same that we mean by the same word figuratively used. The very general acceptance of Christian ideas, principles, convictions, of Christian ways of looking at things, of Christian standards of right and wrong, has been a marked and continuous feature in the history of the world since the Kingdom of Heaven was preached, and is more marked now than ever. The "three measures of meal" of which our Lord speaks[1] have been taken to mean the three continents of Asia, Europe, and Africa, which geographically, and historically too, hang together. That is not so artificial as it might

---

[1] Matt. xiii. 33.

seem at first sight, because our Lord (as man) knew of these three and of no more. Moreover, the influence of Christianity has, in fact (with very slight exceptions, which do not seem destined to be permanent), been confined to the inhabitants of those three continents and their descendants in other lands. Our Lord may quite well have intended to convey to us the assurance that all the populations of the three continents should be "leavened" by Christianity. The three measures of meal represent the dull inert masses upon which Christianity has to exert its influence. The *hiding* of the leaven points to the great truth that Christian influences must spread from within, not be imposed from without : that they work by means of contact, and the most successfully when with the least observation. Nothing could be truer in the mission field, for example, than the saying that the Kingdom of Heaven cometh not with observation. It is an enormous hindrance to British missions that what they strive to recommend is the religion of an alien, a dominant, a much-observed and closely - scrutinized race. It is an almost equal hindrance that they are worked with such an apparatus, so much machinery, so much advertisement. The ideal missionary is one who is completely "hidden," who is in all respects but his Christianity on an absolute level with those among whom he works, who excites no suspicions, exacts no deference, causes no sense of aloofness. It is precisely the " observation " which inevitably attends the white man, the European, the creature of another world, of a higher civilization, of more complicated

necessities, which hinders the Kingdom from coming.
For the leaven is not anything different from the
mass into which it is inserted. It is simply a piece
of the same which has already taken on this peculiar
state of fermentation, and is used to induce the same
state in the rest. It is the action of like upon like,
and all it needs is close contact under the average
conditions of temperature. The fragment of dough
which is fermenting has the property of setting up a
similar fermentation in the midst of the great mass
of dough which lies around it. All religious propa-
gandas which are really successful work this way.
The primitive Christianity, *e.g.*, of the first ages ; or
the Anabaptist doctrine which spread so rapidly and
secretly throughout central Europe in the first quarter
of the sixteenth century. Many people, who have
only heard of the delusions and excesses of the
Anabaptists, may be surprised at finding them
placed side by side with primitive Christians. But,
indeed, their enthusiasm was at first a genuinely
Christian one (however mistaken in some things),
and the methods by which they spread resembled
with a singular closeness those of the first days.
They belonged exclusively to the class of workers
from whom our Lord drew His disciples. It was
easy for them to go about, because they could
support themselves at their trade, and the very fact
that they had a trade gave them an introduction
everywhere. Trades unions flourished then—as they
also did, no doubt, in the apostolic age — under
another name, and fellow craftsmen drew together
very easily. The Anabaptist missionary tramped on

foot with a few clothes and books tied up in a bundle
with the tools of his craft.   His wife tramped beside
him (just as St. Peter's wife may have done), carrying,
perhaps, a baby on her back, and leading a child by
the hand.   If they were caught she shared his death,
as she had shared his life.   But they were not
generally caught.   There is no concealment like
being lost in a great crowd, and no access to the
many like being as poor as themselves.   The
Anabaptist missionary made shoes, maybe—as St.
Paul made tents; and as he sat and worked from
dawn to dusk in some mean close workshop he had
the ear of the man beside him, as no one else could.
And his wife had the same opportunity in the field
or over the wash-tub.   Were they not brothers and
sisters already, in adversity, in poverty, in oppression?
There were no good things for any of *them* in this
world: only contempt, and toil, and hunger, and
possibly the sword.   Yet if the Kingdom of God
came, and all good folk were *really* brothers and
sisters, then, indeed, it would be happy to live and
happier still to die.   And then the well-thumbed
Testament or the Anabaptist tract would come out
of some inner pocket; and the man would sit with
his awl in his hand and listen open-mouthed to a
Gospel which was a Gospel indeed—a Gospel for the
poor.   The woman, too, at the tub would wipe the
sweat off her face with a soapy hand while she
listened to the simple talk of the kindly stranger
wife from far away, who told her of a Christian
fellowship in which all were equal and all loved
one another.   Thus silently, secretly, swiftly, the

contagion of Anabaptist opinion spread to every
town in Germany, and laid hold upon a large part
of the population before ever men knew. And thus
—almost exactly thus—had Christianity spread,
especially after the growing jealousy of the Empire
put a stop to the public preaching of the word. The
leaven was well "hidden"—in the very heart of the
great cities and of the lower classes—and worked
there all the more effectively. The Kingdom came
quickly and surely, just because it was not with
observation.

It is evident enough, from a somewhat different
point of view, that the parable not only illustrates
very wonderfully the process by which Christian
ideas spread, but also very accurately the results
of that process. It is of course opinion, belief,
conviction, which spreads from mind to mind. The
mass is "leavened," *i.e.*, it passes into a state which
is different and to an indefinite degree better. The
process does not stop until the whole is leavened.
Christian ideas and ideals are undoubtedly taking
hold of the world, and there are few countries where
they have not already a certain acceptance. The
rulers and people of Japan, *e.g.*, are in the mass
distinctly unchristian ; yet they have indirectly taken
over from Christianity, through what is called western
civilization, a number of Christian ideas and principles. Even Mohammedan countries are slowly
yielding to the Christian feeling against slavery
and polygamy. How much this sort of thing
may be worth it is impossible to say, but it is
equally impossible not to rejoice at any extension
of the ethical principles of Christianity. It is, how-

ever, absurd to confound, as some do, the acceptance
of certain Christian ideas with Christianity. The
leavening process will go on until the whole world
is more or less affected by Christian opinion, and
it will be a matter of rejoicing; but it will not
mean that all people will be Christians in any
reasonable sense. For *that* the two processes of
growth must go on equally, each in its own way.
Men must become members of the one body, as
well as become animated by one spirit. As it is,
the two processes are most strangely separated.
Many who cling devoutly to the visible fellowship
of the Saints are almost untouched by the influence
of Christian ideals, or even of moral earnestness.
Many more who have abandoned and even scouted
Christianity as a religion, and have no name or
place in the Christian Church, show no disposition
to shake off the effects and influences of a lofty
Christian morality. Not unfrequently they remain
under the spell of their old spiritual environment,
and are unmistakably Christian in their tone of
thought. Hence arises endless confusion of thought
and speech, as to who and what *is* Christian, who
and what *is not*. The Kingdom of Heaven is like
unto *both* things—the mustard-tree and the leaven—
different and indeed contrasted as they are. It will
be our wisdom to recognize it in both aspects; our
privilege to rejoice over its manifestations in both,
and to anticipate the time when, each manifestation
being perfect, the two will coalesce, and there shall
be in all the world *one* Body of Christ animated
in every member by *one* Spirit, and having the
same mind which was in Him.

VI.

THE PARABLE OF THE HID TREASURE

St. Matthew xiii. 44.

· Again, the kingdom of heaven is like unto treasure hid in a field ;
the which when a man hath found, he hideth, and for joy thereof goeth
and selleth all that he hath, and buyeth that field.

IN passing from one parable of the Kingdom to
another, we are more often struck with a keen
sense of contrast than anything else. In a moment
we find ourselves transported into another world of
imagery, of thought, of doctrine. Surely no one
can have dwelt with any sort of intelligence upon
these parables without being shaken and startled
out of that narrowness of view which so naturally
besets religion. These seven are set forth with a
certain equality, as though no one could claim pre-
eminence over the rest, far less exclusive possession
against them. Yet they represent totally diverse
aspects of Christianity. It is, perhaps, impossible
for anyone to feel anything like an equal interest in
all these aspects. It is rare for anyone to feel any
real interest at all in every one of them. Natural
temperament has much to do with the choice which
we actually make, and the general drift of our

religious training determines the rest. Thus for a great multitude of Christians the Kingdom of Heaven is either the stately and astonishing growth of a Society, or it is the rapid and pervasive spread of Christian ideas; possibly these two things blend in their thoughts. In other words they are content with the Mustard Tree and the Leaven. These interest them; the rest they accept without interest and almost without intelligence. For another multitude the mystical side of Christianity is everything: what it brings to them personally in the way of a peculiar and a priceless possession, filling them with a boundless satisfaction. For them the Kingdom is a Hid Treasure, or a Pearl of great price.

It is indeed hardly possible to exaggerate the immensity of the transition from the leaven to the treasure. For, obviously, the leaven is an influence, spreading secretly but surely by contact, by contagion. Different as it is from the tree, it is yet alike in this—that it deals with mankind in masses. It may, and does, affect them one by one; but this is not the point. Essentially it communicates to them a certain condition, brings them into a certain state, which is general and tends to be universal: "Till it was *all* leavened." It is this note of catholicity which is common to the tree and the leaven. The tree is an organized corporate body, drawing up surrounding materials into itself and making them part of itself by virtue of its own peculiar life. The leaven superinduces its characteristic state upon all that it finds to work upon. The

note of the treasure and the pearl is also oneness;
not the oneness of a common life or a common
state, but the oneness of a solitary and incom-
municable possession. This is not only different,
but opposed—so strictly opposed that only in the
Kingdom of Heaven could the two things co-exist.
We know perfectly well that the man who finds
the treasure is not going to share it with anyone
else. Even less is he who buys the pearl going
to let other people wear it. There is no law against
it, of course. The owner of the treasure may endow
a hospital with it if he pleases, or spend it in feasting
the neighbourhood. *If he pleases*—but you know
he will not. You know he will not, because our
Lord makes it clear by one of His most characteristic touches. When this man chanced to find out
that such a treasure *was*, in fact, buried in the field,
he did not go and tell anyone else; he did not
congratulate the owner on the wealth which properly
belonged to him; he did not form a company to
buy the field at a fair price. He "hid" the treasure
found, *i.e.*, he kept his discovery dark, gave no hint
that the field was anything better than its neighbours;
bid for it, and bought it in a casual, careless way,
as though he wanted it for building on or to make
a brickfield of. That was odious—or at the least
was objectionable. And there is not anything more
noticeable in our Lord's parables than His entire
indifference to the moral character of those whom
we might call the "heroes" of His stories. The
very people whom He sets up for us to take example
by, whom He selects to illustrate the essential

characters of His Kingdom, are people whom we
are bound to reprobate most strongly *on His own
principles*. The Unjust Steward is one of these
"heroes," and he is admittedly odious. But the
Wise Virgins are not less odious in reality. The
man who bought a field, concealing the fact that
it contained a treasure, was fraudulent. The king
who sentenced a wedding guest to a horrid fate
because he was not properly dressed was cruel.
We must see clearly why this is if we are to
understand the nature of a parable. The reason
is that the character of these personages does not
come into question at all, nor their conduct, save
in some one particular. They are illustrations,
examples, drawn quite fresh from common life
without any alteration or extenuation. That is
their charm and their force. They are absolutely
natural. In real life most men are more or less
dishonest—or at any rate fail in straightforwardness
—under sufficient temptation. So they are in the
parables. In real life, as a rule, the successful are
not generous, and the powerful are not just; neither
are they in the parables. It makes the parable
vastly more realistic, and it serves to concentrate
attention upon the true purport of it. The parable
is magnificent as a means of teaching, precisely
because it is so limited. The moral inferiority of
the characters introduced forces this limitation upon
our notice. That fact will come out with peculiar
plainness when we reach some later parables, in
which the actors have a good deal to say and to
do.

Meanwhile, we are quite sure that the man who found the treasure, being in fact of a covetous and somewhat unscrupulous disposition, had no thought whatever of sharing his treasure. His one thought was to make it legally and securely his own by the purchase of the field. In this aspect of the Kingdom it is an individual possession; it belongs, whole and entire, to the one who has the happiness to make it his own, and there is no thought of sharing it. That it may be the common property of millions we know from other parables; we could not possibly have guessed it from this. It is the very object of this similitude to banish everybody else from the field of vision. Here is the fortunate individual, and here is the treasure. The man possesses himself of the treasure—with carefulness, with joy, at a great price—that is all. We *must* ask, we *must* know, what the treasure is. What is it, of which the individual Christian may and does possess himself if he is happy enough to become aware of it and eager enough to pay the necessary price? There is not really any doubt, nor has there ever been. The mystics of all ages have returned the same unhesitating answer, from St. Paul and St. John downwards. Our Lord taught the same truth before them. In His deepest utterances He always proposes HIMSELF as the only adequate and final object of our spiritual desire and ambition. Other things are of course mentioned; treasure in Heaven, eternal life, the resurrection from the dead, and so on. But these are all included in Himself as the supreme gift bestowed upon the souls which believe

G

and love. If it is the religious craving of the soul
to be *fed*, *He* is the living Bread which came down
from Heaven ; if to be *illuminated*, *He* is the Light of
the world, the Light of life, the Sun of Righteousness;
if to *advance* onwards and forwards towards God, *He*
is the Way, and the Door, and the Access to the
Father. He meets us here in Scripture in a hundred
different ways, always saying, " I, I Myself, am what
you want and all you need ; having Me you have all
things, you are rich beyond the dreams of avarice, you
sit already at the right hand of God." Amongst
innumerable promises we may take the one (so
typical and characteristic) made in Rev. ii. 28 to him
that overcometh—" I will give him the morning star."
That sounds, as soon as we hear it, as charming as
it is unexpected. There is only one morning star
(the planet Venus when it shines in the east before
sunrise) ; and that is, in its way, just *the* most
radiantly beautiful thing in all the realm of nature.
It is the very emblem, too, of heavenly purity. It is
impossible to think of the morning star being
smirched or discoloured. Then, too, it shines in all
its beauty, at once soft and brilliant, for hours at
a time ; and yet hardly anyone ever sees it, because
hardly any will be at the pains to get up before
sunrise for the purpose. What, then, does this
" morning star "—our Lord's gift to "him that overcometh "—really mean ? He answers the question
Himself in chapter xxii. 16, and therefore there
cannot be any other adequate answer. "*I* am the
bright and morning star." That explains, of course,
how He can give the morning star (which is one

only, and quite separate and unique) to each of the myriads that overcome. Christ is not divided, but makes Himself over, wholly and entirely, to each of the souls that can and will receive Him.

In the same way *He* is the hid treasure, and *He* the pearl of great price. There may be other explanations, not untrue. But they can only be partial, provisional, inadequate. For beyond all question he that overcometh—that overcometh his disinclination, his repugnance, to give up everything else for the Kingdom of Heaven's sake—shall have the treasure, the pearl, the morning star ; and each of these is Christ—nothing else, nothing less. No doubt this is the teaching of the mystics, and by many Christians whatever savours of mysticism is suspected and abhorred. But it is not possible to get rid of Christian mysticism as long as we receive the testimony of St. John and St. Paul, and (yet more) of our Lord Himself. When a man like St. Paul, *e.g.*, is moved to speak—as he sometimes does — out of the fulness of his heart about his own religious convictions and aspirations, we know that we have got behind all his sermons and his arguments ; we have got to the secret spring and source of his religious life. We know this when we hear him saying to the Philippians, " I count all things to be loss for the excellency of the knowledge of Christ Jesus my Lord : for whom I suffered the loss of all things, and do count them but dung, that I may gain Christ, and be found in Him."[1] We may well suppose that when he penned those words he

[1] Phil. iii. 8, 9.

was actually thinking of the merchant who had
bought and who valued a number of other pearls,
goodly enough in their way; but when he found
the one sold all the rest, and was more than content
to part with them in order to secure the one of great
price. For him the pearl and the treasure could
not possibly have meant (in the final truth of things)
anything but Christ—Christ to be his by an identity
of interests, of possessions, of life. "I live; yet no
longer I, but Christ liveth in me."[1]   With this agrees
absolutely that saying of St. John, with which he
sums up as it were all his theology: "The witness
is this, that God gave unto us eternal life, and this
life is in His Son."[2]   Therefore it follows as of
course, "He that hath the Son hath the life, he
that hath not the Son of God hath not the life."[3]
Mysticism it is, beyond all question.   But it is quite
definite and simple in its way.   Christianity in the
ultimate truth of it means Christ.   His gifts, His
glories, His life are not separate from Himself.   It
is not only *through* Him, or *by* Him, or *with* Him,
but *in* Him that all things are to be reconciled to
the Father, and restored to the perfect unity and
harmony of the new creation.

Nothing is more noteworthy in the records of
Christianity than the way in which this aspect of
the Kingdom has asserted itself.   It has had a
separate history.   It has run in channels of its own.
It has been most cherished by isolated individuals,
or groups of individuals, especially in the darkest

---

[1] Gal. ii. 20.   [2] 1 John v. 11.
[3] *Ibid.* 12.

days of the Kingdom. When the visible Church was at once everything and nothing; *everything* in the way of self-assertion, of ambition, of worldliness —as though the powers of the world to come had exhausted themselves in the development of an earthly hierarchy; *nothing* in the way of spiritual help and consolation; then men fell back upon the mystical side of Christianity and found it sufficient for them. St. Bernard of Clairvaux was not altogether contrary to the dominant Churchmanship of his time; in some ways he largely influenced it. But we are certain that he found no spiritual comfort in it. His own religion is expressed in his hymns, and is summed up in the holy Name. His inner life was completely dominated by the passionate longing, not for the gifts of Christ, but for Christ Himself. " My Beloved is mine and I am His " had only one meaning for him, just as it has only one meaning for us.

The German mystics, the Friends of God, the Brethren of the Common Life (to whom Thomas à Kempis belonged) were all in the same case. Some, indeed, were perfectly orthodox, and lived in quiet submission to Rome; some rebelled more or less openly and were bitterly persecuted. They had this in common (and it was the crucial point) that they regarded with comparative indifference the other aspects of the Kingdom, and fixed their eyes upon its most inward and spiritual truth. The apparent hopelessness of the times helped to force this upon them. Nothing seemed to be sown anywhere but tares. The mustard tree was very big, but had become the abode of every filthy and ravenous bird and of nothing else. The ideas and principles of Christ seemed to be totally forgotten or perverted. Well, the hid treasure, the pearl of price was still there for any individual whose eyes were opened to recognize it, whose heart was whole to make it his own. The purely personal aspect of the Kingdom, in which there are only two persons concerned, in which every other creature and every other consideration is excluded save only Jesus and the soul, *that* was the aspect which remained for men, which gained even a new significance and importance, as the night seemed to deepen around them. The thoughts, the books even, of this period are those which have had the most abiding influence. The *Imitation of Christ* is far from being perfect (its limitations indeed are obvious), but of all uninspired writings it has been the most widely effective, because it is the most simple and beautiful presentment of this aspect of the Kingdom. It does not require much study of religious history, although it *does* require a certain resolute openness of mind, to recognize the fact that this supreme truth of the Kingdom has been known and cherished in all quarters otherwise most diverse and opposed. Its predominance cannot apparently be connected with anything else in the way of religion. We might have supposed that it would have been largely found among the Reformed, who cast off the yoke of the dominant Church. That was not, however, the case. With the exception of Luther none of the leaders had any particular sympathy with the mystical side of Christianity. The doctrinal, the polemical, aspect of religion swallowed up everything. It is on the other side of the field that one must look for that personal love of the Saviour, for that joy in the finding and possessing Him, which is the secret of the treasure and the pearl. Even in the England of Elizabeth there is more of it to be found among the persecuted Romanists than anywhere else. With all his faults and failures Pole would seem to have had more of it than Cranmer. Nothing is more astonishing than the wonderful success of that very unexpected movement which we call the Counter-Reformation, save the paltry and stupid reasons which people are content to give for that success. The few English writers who give any attention to the sweeping victories of the new Romanism are content to ascribe them either to *political* causes (the tyranny of Austria and Spain, etc.), or to *ecclesiastical* causes (the fierce energy of the Papacy, and the indefatigable labours of the Jesuits). It is strange that any really religious mind should rest content with reasons so obviously inadequate. People are not made religious or devout by force ; ecclesiastical activity does not produce profound spiritual results. There must have been some power much greater than those assigned in order to account for the wholesale return of people to the Roman obedience. Probably the cause was a very simple one, and has only been overlooked because it was purely religious. It is hardly too much to say that for the Reformers of the second generation theology was everything

and the personal Saviour nothing; at any rate it
would only be the exaggeration of a very melancholy
truth. An endless minuteness of theological defini-
tion, an everlasting insistence upon the dogmatic
(or, we may say, intellectual) side of faith is after
all only husks for hungry souls. In measure, and
in place, it belongs to the Kingdom; but it is not
all, or the most necessary. The fatal error of the
Reformation—at any rate on the Continent, after
the first ardour of it was past—was just this, that
it did *not* offer the Saviour to people as the treasure
and the pearl. It offered them the dogma of justification by faith only; it offered them controversial
statements (chiefly negative) on a hundred different
points; but, to put it quite simply, it did *not* offer
them the living Saviour to be loved, adored, and
above all to be possessed. And that was just
what the great religious teachers of the Counter-
Reformation did. In their doctrine men and women,
whose religious needs and instincts were after all
the same as ours, saw Jesus stretching out His arms
to them and bidding them come to Him that they
might be really His and He be really theirs. And
that told; not of course with all, or nearly all, for
a large proportion of Christians are not moved by
what is admittedly a mystical aspect of the faith;
but with all the more simple and devout.

Political pressure and ecclesiastical activity no doubt
added much to the overwhelming success of such
men as St. Carlo Borromeo of Milan, and St. Francis
de Sales, but the main cause of their success was
that they preached Christ as a treasure which a man

might really acquire. Bitterly disappointed with
the utter failure of mere *doctrine* (however much
it might claim to be founded on the Scriptures) to
give inward peace and security, men returned in
crowds to the old system pressed upon them with
such new persuasiveness. They swallowed its
dogmas (perverse and false as they largely were)
with more or less reluctance and dislike, because
there was about it a wonderful glow and warmth of
heavenly love, the love of Christ which constraineth.
No one but a theological student would ever dream of
opening the books written by the Protestant controversialists of that period ; they are dust and ashes
to the soul. Thousands and thousands, who utterly
reject the whole Papal system, find delight and comfort in the writings of St. Francis de Sales. It will
appear true that it is more hopeful to preach the most
faulty kind of religion, *with* a living Saviour in it,
than the most correct kind *without.* In other words,
Christianity will never hold the souls of men unless
it include a strong mystical element. In yet other
words, the Kingdom is hopelessly incomplete unless
it be presented in its inmost truth as the treasure
and the pearl. If we bear that in mind, it will account
for a great many religious phenomena, both in the
past and in the present, which popular explanations
(mostly of the shallowest) entirely fail to explain.

VII

THE PARABLE OF THE PEARL OF GREAT PRICE.

St. Matthew xiii. 45, 46.

Again, the kingdom of heaven is like unto a merchant man, seeking goodly pearls : who, when he had found one pearl of great price, went and sold all that he had, and bought it.

THERE is no discernible difference between this parable and the one immediately preceding, except in a single point. All the rest—the discovery, the joy, the readiness to part with everything else, the acquisition—are the same. As to these the only thing that anyone could suggest is that the second parable indicates more pointedly the eagerness of search which preceded the discovery. The merchant was undoubtedly engaged in seeking goodly pearls ; he had made a speciality of that search and pursued it with enthusiasm. The other man *may* have become aware of the treasure quite accidentally ; or he may have long suspected the existence of some such thing and been looking for it. Anyhow, his joy when he did know of it may be set off against the other's eagerness to find. But in one point the contrast is sharp and very instructive. The pearl was itself for sale, the treasure was not. The pearl could be had (at a great price) straightway, the treasure could only be had as included in the field. In the one case the sacrifice is joyfully made, really and truly for the treasure, but seemingly and in outward form for the field. In the other case any such complication is unnecessary and excluded. Now if this minor and incidental contrast were not substantiated by Christian experience, it might be put aside as belonging merely to the picturesque detail of the parable. Such details are often over-pressed. But Christian experience *does* emphatically substantiate the contrast as one which runs right down the centuries and reappears in all lands and ages. The witness of the Spirit and the Bride is this. The treasure and the pearl are alike Christ. To "find" Christ, to "gain" Christ, to "possess" Christ, to "have" Christ for his very own, is the ultimate truth of the Kingdom for all that have really grasped its significance. But here comes a difference. For some He is a treasure indeed, but hid in the field of the Word and Sacraments. Their enthusiasm, their self-sacrifice, are devoted to this end, that they may make the field theirs; but only for the sake of the treasure which it contains.

For others, again, He is apprehended, and it is impossible to doubt that He is made their own, apart from anything else, irrespective of any means of grace. In a broad sense it is open to us to call this the contrast between the sacramental and the non-sacramental aspects of Christianity, both of which are sufficiently conspicuous in the Bible, in Christian history, and in Christian experience. The evil is that people find it so difficult to believe in both. The man who has sacrificed everything for the pearl charges his brother with folly in spending his all on a field which is worth so little, which can be

characterized by so many disparaging epithets. Yet
the field contains for him (not in his own opinion, but
in truth) the identical treasure which the other has in
his pearl. On the other hand the man who has with
joyful self-surrender made the field his own is unable
to believe that the other's pearl can indeed be the
equivalent of his hidden treasure. Why not? Is it
not obvious that the whole sacramental system,
inasmuch as it belongs to the grace of our Lord
Jesus Christ, has only a *positive* significance. It has
not any negative meaning. It cannot be read backward, or made to condemn. To affirm most
constantly that Christ is found in the sacraments
is not for one moment to assert or to insinuate that
He is not found out of the sacraments. If we say
that *baptized* infants, dying in infancy, are certainly
saved, are we justly accused of holding that
unbaptized infants so dying are certainly lost? Is
not that the hasty conclusion of vulgar souls which
measure the breadth of the Divine charity by their
miserable little earthly footrules? To the same
vulgarity of soul must be ascribed all similar
negative conclusions. We affirm that the Body and
Blood of Christ are verily and indeed taken and
received in the Holy Communion. Is that tantamount to saying that they cannot be received out
of the Holy Communion? God forbid. No one—
no adult at least—can be saved without. "Except
ye eat the flesh of the Son of man, and drink His
blood, ye have not life in yourselves."[1] "He that
eateth My flesh, and drinketh My blood, abideth in

---

[1] John vi. 53.

Me, and I in him."[1] And this is the condition of eternal life. Will anyone affirm that all the many then and since who have lived good and noble and (often) very Christian lives *without* the Holy Sacrament have perished everlastingly? Of course not. They may prefer to get out of the difficulty (as it seems to them) by a most illogical and untheological reference to the "uncovenanted mercies" of God, but they can only acknowledge in effect that there is no grace of Christ to be had in Sacraments which is not to be had also (under certain conditions) out of Sacraments. As to "uncovenanted," no covenant could be expressed in words more reliable, more definite, more conclusive than this: "Whosoever shall call upon the name of the Lord shall be saved":[2] and there are not several kinds of salvation declared in the New Testament, but *one* only, and that *one* by way of being in Christ, and He in us. Neither, again, can anyone seriously think that there are two kinds of Divine forgiveness of sins for Christ's sake, and one kind inferior to the other. It is, of course, precisely and identically the same forgiveness, as blessed and as effectual, whether we go to the priest with a true penitent heart for the absolution which he (for our comfort and assurance) is commissioned to declare, or whether in the same spirit of penitence we look up to the Father who ever waits to be gracious unto us. It is the vulgarity —the meanness and narrowness — which clings to human views of things Divine, which has given such unfortunate currency to these miserable negations and

---

[1] John vi. 56.   [2] Acts ii. 21 ; Rom. x. 13.

oppositions. The sacramental and non-sacramental views of grace are both true. If we deny either we come into hopeless conflict with many things in the Bible, and with a vast mass of Christian experience which no theories can explode, no impatience move out of the way.

It must further be observed, however, that whilst the two men obtained the same prize in somewhat different ways, it was not open to them, in fact, to choose their way. The one could only purchase the field which contained the treasure : the other could only buy the pearl itself. For the majority of Christians, at any rate, the ordinary condition of things is represented by the first. In the pious and devout use of means of grace (whatever these may be) they "find" Christ. They know this field, more or less, from childhood; and if they think it worth the price the field may always be theirs. The question of questions for them is, will they discern the treasure hidden in it? Will they learn to love and value the field, will they care to make it ever-more their own for the sake of the treasure? There is always the danger that they will not, but will end by falling into one or other of two opposite errors— opposite in appearance, though in fact springing out of the same failure : the error of attaching a superstitious importance to the field as if it were valuable apart from the treasure, or the error of abandoning the field as of no value at all. Of those who fail to discern the treasure the more ignorant fall generally into the former error; the better educated into the latter. There does not seem to be much to choose between them. Once, however, a man has realized what there is for *him* in the field, there is not anything he would not do or suffer to get the field and keep it. How many have risked their lives in order to be baptized? How many have forfeited their lives through their eagerness to be partakers of the holy Mysteries? To accuse such of folly, of extravagance, of superstitious regard for externals, would only be an evident token of spiritual blindness and poverty. With the eye of faith these men saw Jesus beckoning to them; with the ear of faith they heard Him calling to them to arise and come to Him: in certain outward ways, indeed, accommodated to their bodily nature, but not the less really and truly; they saw, they heard, they went; and if they lost their lives over it, it only meant that they sold all they had to buy the field— not for the field's sake, but the treasure's. That was how the Kingdom was shown to them, and that was how they took it by force, not counting their lives dear unto them for the Kingdom of Heaven's sake. Nor would it be otherwise now if persecution revived. The extraordinary and undying power which the Sacraments have over the minds of men is not due to any obstinacy of superstition which can be combated by a judicious selection of well-known texts. Those that think so are themselves the victims of a shallow delusion. The fascination of Sacraments is due to the rooted (and well-rooted) conviction that in the use of them is to be found Christ Himself—the hid treasure of His own parable. Nothing can ever argue away this conviction: it is founded on Scripture, on testimony, and on experience, which cannot be set aside. On the other hand the same witness is equally sure and certain in what might seem the opposite sense. Everyone who recognizes the supreme value of Christ can become possessed of Him, if willing to pay the price. Given that willingness, and there is no hindrance. He is quite accessible. It needs no intermediary. One might be absolutely without Church, without Bible, without Christian society, and find no difficulty in coming by the pearl of great price. He is always willing to be ours: and we are always at liberty to part with all that we have for His sake. To all souls that will pray, in the spirit of penitence, humility, self-surrender, and faith, Christ is directly accessible, and not only accessible but obtainable. He is theirs, if they count nothing else dear in comparison with Him. What is so deplorable is that so many people who know this are not content with affirming it, but must go on to deny and denounce the other, and complemental, truth. They rave against sacramentalism and sacerdotalism. They lash themselves into a fury against such as proclaim the means and ministries of grace. They want to narrow down all religious experience to the scanty limits of their own. Yet the facts of spiritual life, which on a large scale are quite unmistakable, tell us plainly that the truth lies on both sides at once. It may be annoying or even humiliating to the pride of human reason and the impatience of human prejudice that it should be so, but so it is. The parable of the treasure hid in the field is not more true than the parable of the pearl, but it is not less true either.

The question, therefore, between the sacramental and the non-sacramental conception of Christianity is futile, because both are true ; neither errs, except in excluding the other. But the question about the one condition which is common to both is immensely important and even pressing. It often looks as if it were shelved by a tacit conspiracy of silence. "Went and sold all that he had" in order to possess himself of the one thing needful, in the one case indirectly, in the other case directly. While we dispute about the directly or indirectly, we all ignore the price. And yet it can have but one significance. Whatever else a man has of property, of happiness, of present possessions, of future prospects, he must be absolutely and heartily willing to give it all up for the sake of "gaining Christ." That is the very least we can make of it. It may be seriously argued that a man should not only be willing to do it, but he should in fact do it. When St. Anthony of Egypt entered the church, and heard the words of the Gospel being read, "Go, sell whatsoever thou hast, and give to the poor, and thou shalt have treasure in heaven," he never doubted that the words applied to him, for he too was very rich—for that age and land. Why not? What was there in the lapse of two centuries to make the command (or invitation rather) inapplicable to Anthony? People take for granted that it is not applicable to rich young men now, but they are not able to give any reason for that convenient assumption except that it *is* convenient. Times and circumstances have changed, they say. If they mean that in detail they have

H

changed, it is a truism and irrelevant. If they mean that in any substantial sense they have changed, it is untrue. Our Lord lived on earth under a settled government, in the midst of a highly civilized community, where money and property held much the same position they do now. The assumption that things are quite different now is entirely (though unconsciously) due to hypocrisy. People do not want to give up anything for religion. On the contrary, they expect religion to increase the comfort and convenience of their lives. So they make believe that these words of our Lord, and the many like unto them, have been cancelled by lapse of time and change of outward conditions. But there is no man can say *why* they should have become obsolete, or *when* they became so. Putting aside these flimsy and hypocritical evasions, it is obvious that nothing at all has ever been cancelled. The utmost that can be said is this, that the invitation to part with everything and to embrace a life of "evangelical poverty" cannot be enforced on anyone from without. There it is, and the rich man is at liberty to take it or leave it. If he take it he will have no less reward than the rich man would have had if he had followed Christ. If he leave it he will suffer the same loss—no more and no less —which *that* man suffered: not the loss of eternal life, or of his "soul," or anything of that kind ; but simply the loss of a possible happiness, of an attainable freedom, in the spiritual life, worth more than all the riches of this world. Nothing really alters or grows out of date in the great issues of

life. Any man nowadays giving up his property
from Christian motives would enjoy the same supernatural peace and joy which so many of the early
disciples enjoyed: he would in no wise lose his
reward. The pearl would be his in a specially
delightsome way. For the rest it is only necessary
to insist on the real willingness and readiness to
give up everything for the sake of Christ. *If* the
call came unmistakably, *if* the necessity arose, could
they and would they cheerfully part with all, and
still think themselves more than rich having *Him?*
The difficulty is to know, even in one's own case,
without having tried. To most people, undoubtedly,
who have means, the prospect of doing without
them seems so blankly intolerable that one feels
the utmost uneasiness on the subject. A small
deprivation presents itself to them as an impossibility, the thought of which cannot be faced.
One wishes devoutly that some rich people would
voluntarily reduce themselves to poverty, just to
show that it can be done. Meantime it is clear
that we ought to realize the gravity of the situation.
We stand accused of a profound hypocrisy. We
are told over and over again that Christ can only
be ours at the price of everything else which we
value. In point of fact we cling to everything else
with a vigilant and eager tenacity, and we claim to
have Christ too. We have so accustomed ourselves
to this attitude (in the very teeth of His words)
that we have got to look upon it as the very essence
of enlightened religion. Nothing could be more
fatal. The one chance we have is to exercise our-

selves continually in an inward renunciation of all
wealth, all happiness, for Christ's sake. It is possible
to detach oneself from all one's belongings, to survey
them, as it were, from without, to realize what the
loss of them would be, and to make an offering
of them all to God—a freewill offering—if it would
please Him. It is possible to regard all one's
belongings as not one's own, as blessings renounced
and only retained from day to day until it please
Him to take them. In such ways one may test
and strengthen one's readiness to part with all that
one has. It is not altogether satisfactory, but it is
the best we can do, short of actually impoverishing
ourselves, and we are bound to do it. The common
attitude of mind, according to which a man clings
to every possession he has to the last possible
minute, and when he cannot keep it any longer
tries to content himself with the thought of having
the heavenly treasure instead, is unspeakably
dreadful. It is only necessary to realize what it
really means to perceive how utterly opposite it is
to the temper depicted in the parable: "*for joy
thereof* goeth and selleth all that he hath, and
buyeth that field."

It is very important to note, in taking leave of
these two parables, that it *is* a temper, not a transaction, which is really intimated in that buying and
selling. Wonderful it is that our Lord can, both here
and elsewhere, use these terms of commerce in connection with the Kingdom of Heaven. St. Paul
could not have done it. And if anyone else but his
Master had done it, he would assuredly have fallen

foul of him.   On the face of it, it is clean contrary
to all that doctrine of the absolute freedom of the
grace of God, and of our utter incapacity in any
way to deserve it or to give any equivalent for it,
which St. Paul preached.   It must have seemed to
him (if he knew of it) extraordinary—one is tempted
to write *unfortunate*—that our Lord should have used
language so calculated to mislead.   That no efforts,
no sacrifices, of our own will procure for us the grace
and favour of God, is so prominent and so perpetual
a theme with all great preachers !   So prominent and
so perpetual indeed that they have created a widespread though undefined conviction that all efforts, all
sacrifices, for the Kingdom of Heaven's sake are to
be regarded with suspicion.   Eternal life is the free
gift of God, which a man is to lay hold of by faith
alone apart from works.   Why then should there
be any talk of making sacrifices in order to gain
Christ?   It is indeed notable, the perfect uncon-
sciousness of any such theological difficulty which
confronts us in our Lord's words, both first and
last.   For it is the same in His message to the
Church in Laodicea, " I counsel thee to *buy* of Me
gold."[1]   The doctrine of free grace, of salvation by
faith apart from works, is of course absolutely true.
So is this other doctrine of the necessary readiness
to sacrifice everything.   The reconciliation may or
may not be easy.   It makes little difference.   What
is important is not the theoretical reconciliation of
complemental truths, but the practical holding of
them fast, however much they seem to differ.

[1] Rev. iii. 18.

But it is at least evident that what is insisted on is not a transaction, a bargain between the seeker and the sought, but a temper in the seeker. He is to be so thoroughly in earnest that he will stick at no surrender so as he may attain his end. He may in fact have nothing to part with; he may not be asked to part with anything: but the readiness must be there; he must be in that mind about it, that it will be a joy to him to let anything and everything go so he may possess the treasure, the pearl. We shall see abundantly hereafter that one chief object of the parables of the Kingdom is to inculcate *tempers*, not to intimate *transactions*.

VIII

THE PARABLE OF THE DRAG-NET

St. Matthew xiii. 47–50.

Again, the kingdom of heaven is like unto a net, that was cast into the sea, and gathered of every kind : which, when it was full, they drew to shore, and sat down, and gathered the good into vessels, but cast the bad away. So shall it be at the end of the world : the angels shall come forth, and sever the wicked from among the just, and shall cast them into the furnace of fire : there shall be wailing and gnashing of teeth.

AGAIN a contrast, a transition, so great as to confound our thoughts for the time. It is like suddenly opening a door and passing into an atmosphere so different that at first we can hardly breathe. Whatever we have said or thought about the previous parables is no use to us here. We have been dealing with the question of choice, individual choice, the choice upon which everything hangs. And now there is not any choice at all. The fishes in the net represent souls—that is certain —but the most outstanding feature of the situation is that the fishes never exercised any volition whatever. As far as they are concerned their presence there is absolutely accidental. They were not consulted, nor invited, nor attracted. The fisherman who uses rod and line does at least employ the persuasion of a bait. That thought has sometimes

been read into our Lord's saying, "I will make you
fishers of men," as though they were to bait their
hooks with the proffer of eternal life. But that is
untenable, for the Apostles used nets, chiefly if not
exclusively. And the net simply encloses the fish
which happen to be within a certain area. Doubtless
the fishermen let down their nets where they fancy
a shoal may be lying, but the fishes have nothing
whatever to say to it. Is there such an aspect of
the Kingdom in point of fact? At first thought
we should have denied it. It seems so incompatible
with the revealed character of the Kingdom from
all other points of view. There is something so
arbitrary, wholesale, promiscuous in the sweep of
the drag-net ; from the point of view of the fishes
so accidental and involuntary, that we can see
nothing Christian about it. Nevertheless, it is
exactly what has happened.

Historical Christianity, as viewed from without—
for statistical purposes, e.g.—is more like the drag-net
than anything else. People may make what definitions of religion they like, but when they come to
take a religious census (as in estimating the number
of Christians in India) they can only count heads.
They are within the Kingdom who return themselves,
or are returned by their parents, as Christians. If
we consider them it is in most cases a pure accident
—as far as they individually are concerned—that
they are Christian. The enormous majority of
Christians are so by hereditary descent ; and there
is every reason to believe that very few of them
would have embraced Christianity had it demanded

individual conversion and personal effort. There
is nothing harsh or sarcastic in such a statement.
Facts are quite conclusive that the great mass of
mankind everywhere follow the religious profession
of their parents and neighbours. Where anything
like wholesale conversion has taken place it has been
where the hereditary religious feeling has been greatly
weakened by exceptional causes, and where the new
faith has had an unusually powerful backing. In
a word, the immense majority of professing Christians
have exercised little more, if any more, choice in
the matter than the fishes in the drag-net. They
happen to be enclosed within the sweep of the Gospel
drag-net; it is no doing of theirs. They may learn
to praise and bless God for it, but they can only
ascribe it to His good Providence. There is another
thing which we cannot avoid seeing, strange and
uncomfortable as it is. The fishes within the net
are neither better nor worse than those outside.
They are, as it says, "of every kind." Broadly
speaking they only differ from the rest of their
kith and kin by the fact (with all that depends upon
it) of being within the net. Christians at large are
no better and no worse than the rest of mankind,
except so far as the fact of being Christians and
under a certain pressure of Christian opinion has
affected them for good. It is useless to pretend
to ourselves that it is otherwise. The average of
human character is singularly level through all the
great religions of the world, Christianity included.
The stern testimony of facts compels us to acknowledge that this is true, however much we know that

it is not all the truth. We may take any ethical
standard we like which is not *distinctively* Christian,
and apply it to the nations of the world; we shall
find that while they vary greatly in detail they are
much of a muchness on the whole. The fish inside
the net only differ from the others by being inside.
Now what does this mean, religiously? It means
that the great mass of Christians are such, not by
their own choice or wish, but by the election of
God. Not differing in any way that we can tell
from the rest of mankind, they were born of
Christian parents, in Christian lands, are counted
as Christians in the statistics of religion, are subjected
to various Christian influences. Other aspects of the
Kingdom, totally different, may open out before
them as they go on, but this is the most certain
and primary of all. It raises very grave questions,
which we shrink from answering, but it is the most
obvious of all true things in the visible Church;
and the Kingdom of Heaven in this aspect of it
is clearly identical with the visible Church. What
St. Augustine and his friends erroneously deduced
from that other parable of the good and evil seed,
they quite rightly deduced from this. The effort
to form a Christian Society which shall consist
entirely of good people, or converted people, is
bound to end in failure. It is impossible to get
rid of the hypocrites, of the self-deceivers, of those
whose moral sense is undeveloped, of those who go
morally astray and cannot be made to see it. No
doubt the open and flagrant offenders like the man
at Corinth can be cut off, and ought to be. St. Paul

will insist on that being done. But how is St. Paul
himself to cast out "the covetous man who is an
idolater?" Covetousness is in the heart. It is a
greed which poisons all the mind, and injuriously
affects all the conduct. But it only now and then
betrays itself in a wrongful deed of which an ecclesiastical court can take any cognizance; and in a
cautious man, living in a complicated society like
ours, it would probably never so betray itself at
all. If we try to go beyond flagrant cases of offence
against the sixth, seventh, and eighth command-
ments, we shall be certain to retain in our Society
of virtuous Christians some people who are distinctly
worse (and felt to be worse) than those whom we
cast out. We shall quite easily get rid of the
publican and the harlot; we shall have to put up
with the Pharisee, the Sadducee, the Herodian, who
are even further from the Kingdom if the truth be
told.

We fall back then upon the drag-net. The
Church is a world - wide Society for holy living;
but as far as we and they are concerned, it is an
accident who belongs to it. The election is of God.
It is of His will that certain lands are Christian,
that the children of Christians are Christian too
in a certain true and important sense. We do not
pretend that they are better than others—than
Mahometan or Buddhist children, *e.g.* — but they
are better off, and for that we thank God. Nor
can we venture to discern between them; we see
generally that they are "of every kind," like those
outside; but the separation of the bad from the

good must be left to the judgment of God, which it were useless or mischievous to forestall. Now this is, as anyone may see, that aspect of the Kingdom of Heaven which is reflected in the constitution of the Anglican Church, and acted upon in her baptismal services. It is not the *only* aspect—that should go without saying—but it is *a true aspect*, and the one which must be put foremost in a national Church. The baptism of infants belongs to this aspect of the Kingdom, and has no other justification. It seems absurd that baptism, which was meant to seal the solemnest and most personal of all choices, should be administered to babes who have nothing to say in the matter. But then our Lord affirmed most distinctly that " of such is the Kingdom of Heaven," and we know of no other method of admission to the Kingdom but by baptism. At any rate, they cannot be in the visible Church except by baptism, and it seems impossible to keep them out in the face of our Lord's teaching. They belong to the Kingdom (or the Kingdom to them) precisely in this aspect of it which we are considering—as a drag-net. Not by any will of their own, but by His grace and election, they *are*, in fact, Christian. Whatever they are going to be, they do just now by universal consent belong to the Kingdom in a sense, and in a sense which is reflected in the visible Church. Their baptism as infants expresses that fact; it acknowledges the Divine election to the name and standing and privilege of Christians; it accepts and registers the choice, not of man, but of God. What the relation may be

between infant baptism and the new birth which
the sacred writers so often associate with adult
baptism, is a far more difficult matter to determine
than eager partisans, on this side or on that, are
willing to allow. But quite apart from that it is
clear that the baptism of infants stands or falls
with the parable of the drag - net and the saying,
" Of such is the Kingdom of Heaven." Babies (as
such) *can* only have to do with the Kingdom so
far as it is a net, including all within a certain area,
without choice on their part, without moral discrimination on the part of the net. It is God's
will, God's election to grace, God's unexplained
and unchallenged goodness towards the unconscious
child which is humbly accepted and thankfully
registered in infant baptism. If people object to
this baptism, it is (as a rule) because they do not
believe that the Kingdom really has any such
aspect. They cannot find it compatible with the
other and more personal aspects of it. One need
not be surprised. The apparent incongruity is
exceeding great. But it is wonderfully reassuring
to find that the incongruity is just as marked in
the undeniable facts of Christian history as in the
parables of the Kingdom. We are compelled oftentimes, whether we like it or no, to think and speak
of Christianity as though it were a net cast at
random into the sea, which gathered of every kind
without discrimination.

The want of discrimination, however, in the
present condition of the Kingdom, the impossibility
of really successful discrimination in the visible

Church, is balanced in the parable by the severance of the last day. All that we have to call attention to here is the obvious fact that our Lord's teaching about it is intentionally rudimentary. The fishermen "sat down and gathered the good into vessels, but the bad they cast away," not troubling themselves indeed what became of them since they were useless. "The angels shall come forth" from the Heavenly Presence, "and sever the wicked from among the righteous, and shall cast them into the furnace of fire." Is it not evident that the interpretation is almost as purely "pictorial" as the parable itself? No one believes that the awful work of final and eternal discrimination will be left to angels. "We shall all stand before the judgment-seat of Christ."[1] God Himself must "judge the world by that Man whom He hath appointed."[2] The soul must see itself in the light of the Divine holiness, and accept its own inevitable destiny. No creature may come between the Creator and the individual soul in that supreme moment of its endless life. It is only the merest outsides of the tremendous facts and issues of that day which can possibly be committed to the ministry of angels. We understand, therefore, that here (as in so many other places) our Lord does not choose to lift the veil from things to come. He has resort, therefore, to the conventional language of His time, which expressed its real ignorance, its apparent knowledge, in terms of angels.

[1] Rom. xiv. 10.   [2] Acts xvii. 31.

IX

THE PARABLE OF THE UNMERCIFUL SERVANT

St. Matthew xviii. 23–35.

Therefore is the kingdom of heaven likened unto a certain king, which would take account of his servants. And when he had begun to reckon, one was brought unto him, which owed him ten thousand talents. But forasmuch as he had not to pay, his lord commanded him to be sold, and his wife, and children, and all that he had, and payment to be made. The servant therefore fell down, and worshipped him, saying, Lord, have patience with me, and I will pay thee all. Then the lord of that servant was moved with compassion, and loosed him, and forgave him the debt. But the same servant went out, and found one of his fellow-servants, which owed him an hundred pence : and he laid hands on him, and took him by the throat, saying, Pay me that thou owest. And his fellow-servant fell down at his feet, and besought him, saying, Have patience with me, and I will pay thee all. And he would not : but went and cast him into prison, till he should pay the debt. So when his fellow-servants saw what was done, they were very sorry, and came and told unto their lord all that was done. Then his lord, after that he had called him, said unto him, O thou wicked servant, I forgave thee all that debt, because thou desiredst me : shouldest not thou also have had compassion on thy fellow-servant, even as I had pity on thee? And his lord was wroth, and delivered him to the tormentors, till he should pay all that was due unto him. So likewise shall my heavenly Father do also unto you, if ye from your hearts forgive not every one his brother their trespasses.

THIS parable does not belong to either of the two great groups which form such distinctive features of St. Matthew's Gospel. It stands, however, in a somewhat close relation to the parables

of the second group, and is well worth considering
for that reason as well as for its own sake. We
have already seen that the object of a parable may
be to inculcate a temper rather than to intimate
a transaction. And that is altogether the case in
the present instance. Our Lord seems to go out
of His way to tell us that He is talking about the
Kingdom of Heaven. That Kingdom indeed has
been in His mind and the disciples' in their previous
discourse (see chapter xviii. 1–4); but the conversa-
tion has touched on many points since then not
especially connected with it. In verse 23, however,
our Lord proclaims with emphasis that it is the
Kingdom and nothing else that He is going to
speak about. And then He tells them a story which
has no other point whatever than to show how
necessary it is for a Christian to have a forgiving
and a generous temper in the face of wrong and
injury. Thus the Kingdom is identified with a
certain temper—with a virtue which is not at all
distinctively Christian, although it is urged here on
Christian grounds. It is especially important to
grasp this peculiarity here, because it prepares us
to recognize the same thing under more startling
conditions elsewhere. Here, at any rate, it is easy
to allow that our Lord has only one object in view
—to lay stress upon the duty of forgiveness. The
apparatus of the parable (if one may call it so) is
of the simplest. It only exists in order to throw
up into the strongest relief the failure of the
servant to show the kind of temper which is
proper to the Kingdom, and therefore necessary

to salvation. It is not possible to translate the
story as it stands into a Gospel, although of course
it suggests the Gospel. The King of Heaven, whom
we have offended, never commanded us and ours
to be sold—or anything in the least resembling it.
The king in the parable is an earthly monarch pure
and simple, acting upon impulse, at one moment
angry and vindictive, at the next warm-hearted and
generous. In him, as in other men, is good and
evil, but the good triumphs this time, as the evil
might another time. He is of the earth, earthy;
he is only part of the apparatus of the parable.
The whole moral of the story is in the behaviour
of the forgiven servant towards his fellow-servant.
This alone belongs to the Kingdom—or rather is
held up as incompatible with it. The Christian who
has been forgiven so much, forgiven so graciously,
cannot possibly so far forget himself as to show a
vindictive and resentful temper towards his fellows.
If he does, his own forgiveness stands in imminent
danger of being cancelled and withdrawn. The
miserable fate of the unmerciful servant, who has
aroused afresh the wrath of a passionate tyrant, will
find its counterpart in the dreadful destiny of the
unforgiving Christian. Not that our Heavenly
Father can ever be like the king in the parable—
but that it is possible for us to end as the servant
ended.

The Kingdom of Heaven, therefore, is a temper—
from this one particular point of view. It is purely
ethical. It has no connection with Church, or Sacraments, or Preaching, or devotion to a Personal

I

Saviour. It is Christian in motive, because it is the temper of one who knows himself forgiven an immeasurable debt. But it is simply a temper, one that has always been known and admired among men ; one also that is not at all conspicuous among Christian people. It is obvious that our Lord is speaking from an extremely limited and unusual point of view, and that He has very grave reasons for doing so. " The Kingdom of God," says St. Paul, having in mind certain very common and very gross errors, " is not eating and drinking, but righteousness and peace and joy in the Holy Ghost "[1] These things too are ethical ; but they are also spiritual, they belong to the supernatural order, they are in touch with the powers of the world to come. That cannot be said of a forgiving temper. Like courage, chastity, and other virtues, it is common to men, although not common in men. Christian teaching and grace may do much to educate and strengthen it, but they do not create it. All the more remarkable it is that our Lord counts it so absolutely necessary as to identify the Kingdom of Heaven with it. We remember of course that this is far from being the only place where He shows a profound anxiety to force upon us the primary need to have a forgiving temper. He has actually introduced it into the Lord's Prayer, and put it into our own lips. We may not even ask forgiveness without assuring Him that we too forgive, without limiting our own claim upon His mercy by the mercy which we show ourselves. That stands all

[1] Rom. xiv. 17.

alone. In no other respect do we propose ourselves as an example to Him; nor should we dare to do so here if He had not forced it upon us. A really forgiving temper is quite rare, even among sincere Christians; and yet all Christians are obliged to speak to God, Who knows their hearts, as if they forgave all things to all men. We may say with Mr. Ruskin that no one ought to use the Lord's Prayer who is not (in this as in other respects) a consistent follower of Christ. But that comes at once to nought, because there is no authority which can decide the question. Least of all could men undertake to label *themselves* as truly consistent Christians. We must leave the Lord's Prayer to all that, however doubtfully or dolefully, find it in them to say, "Our Father"; and if the prayer itself condemn the greater part of them that use it, we cannot help it. Our Lord has thought it best to put that condemnation into it, because He would by any means force upon our attention the absolute need of a forgiving temper in the Kingdom of Heaven. It is a very strong step to take, so strong as to be almost appalling; but it is only in keeping with all His utterances upon the subject. He never speaks so strongly about anything else.

In the face of this it is an extremely disquieting thing to note how difficult and unpopular a grace this spirit of forgiveness is. Apparently it is even more difficult and unpopular in our own day and country than ever before or anywhere else. The fact has perhaps escaped attention for reasons which will presently appear, but when these reasons are considered it will hardly be denied. If we compare society as it now is (amongst ourselves) with what it was in our Lord's time, we must be aware of two great changes which affect the forgiveness of injuries.

Firstly, society is organized to a great and increasing extent. A man's life is so parcelled out amongst a variety of unions or communities great and small that only a fragment of his life (and that perhaps the least interesting and important) is left him in which to recognize and practise Christian forbearance. To be revengeful, unrelenting, habitually exacting of the uttermost farthing, is, of course, forbidden to a Christian as an individual. But as a citizen, as a member of a syndicate, a federation, a union, he may indulge in all these things ; nay, he is almost bound to. It would be absurd to ask whether any of these unions (whatever their name or constituency) practise Christian forbearance or forgiveness. Their *raison d'être* is to enlarge the profits and to increase the power of their members, and to that end they are inexorable, often unscrupulous, sometimes cruel, in the pursuit of their own policy. Whatever may be said for tradesunions (and no doubt they have done immense good, especially by substituting class-selfishness for that individual selfishness which is so much worse), it is nevertheless a simple fact that their success ultimately rests upon the terror which they inspire. It is a sacred duty among trades-unionists to hate a " blackleg," to heap upon him every species of abuse, to do him any harm that is possible. Of course, the leaders and responsible persons do not commit violence themselves—they ignore it. What they do is by systematic violence of language to produce an atmosphere of intense hatred, out of which every other possible kind of violence is bound to spring. There really is not any doubt about it. One may have an intense sympathy with the workmen as against the employers. One has all the same to confess that the workmen's unions are absolutely merciless towards the only people they really fear—those members, namely, of their own class who cross their purposes by playing (as it seems) into the hands of the employers. Not equally passionate (for there is no temptation), but equally unscrupulous, maybe in a cold, business-like way, are the federations, the syndicates, the trusts, on the other side. Can this be right from a Christian point of view? As a matter of words, people will agree at once that it is not. But they do not see the root of the mischief; they do not see that a man has no right to hand over his conscience to a society, to a union of any sort. As a Christian he is bound by the laws of Christ in all the length and breadth of his life. If the union to which he belongs pursues its ends by means which are merciless, harsh, cruel, he is bound at any cost to himself to quit the union. It may be very difficult to distribute the responsibility for corporate sins against the law of forbearance, but the responsibility exists; a man cannot clear himself of it by pleading that in his private capacity he behaved in a Christian way. Here is one terrible

danger of the present day. Men cut up their lives
into private and public; and the public is by far
the larger and more important of the two; and it
does not even pretend to be regulated by the laws
of Christ.

Secondly, modern life is so admirably "policed,"
and so wonderfully protected from any aggression
of one upon another, that many of us never have
anything to forgive — worth speaking of. In its
way that is a great gain. It puts us under an
enormous obligation to modern civilization, which
takes such care of us and guards our "rights" so
successfully. God forbid that we should regret the
expulsion from our midst of the oppression and
wrong which used to be rampant in most places,
and are still in some. But we have to remember
that we get on so well and comfortably with our
own countrymen, *not* because we and they are good
and kind and considerate, but because we are so
perfectly fenced by law and order that we have
nothing to fear. Life is so minutely arranged for
us (even in crowded cities) that our neighbours
have, as a rule, no chance to injure us; therefore
we get on very fairly well with them. So it has
come to pass that even good people have got into
the way of thinking that their religion is exclusively
personal and domestic; that they may be perfectly
hard and indifferent as against the world at large;
that their duty towards their neighbours is limited
to a vigilant care lest anybody should get any
advantage of them or fail to render to them the
utmost that is due. It is very difficult in practice

to indicate the more excellent way; but it is clear that there lies herein much danger to our souls. The spirit of forbearance, of forgiveness, was never meant to be thus artificially limited. Being so limited as it is it never gets any exercise, and always tends to become weaker and weaker. If we honestly asked ourselves how many injuries we had forgiven during the last twelve months, the answer would be astonishing. After deducting cases of imaginary affront, or of trivial annoyance, we should generally have to confess "we have forgiven nothing, because we had nothing to forgive." But what if we had? What if we had suffered wrong as Christians did in the first ages, as Christians do now in the Turkish Empire? With our keen sense of justice, with our high notion of our own rights, with our long immunity from oppression, could we find it in our hearts to forgive? All the appearances, all the probabilities, are against it. The old Adam within us would rise in wild rebellion against the wrong and the wrong-doer. We should protest with vigour, resist with courage, endure the worst with passionate defiance; but should we be able to forgive? Alas! our very virtues, the virtues of our race which have made it foremost in the world, would all make for failure and condemnation in this respect. Moreover the slight evidences which meet us in daily life are almost all of a disquieting character. It is painful indeed to notice, *e.g.*, how few devout communicants have any notion of really forgiving an injury. It is always just *this* which

they cannot and will not put up with. As long
as they are "let alone," they are exemplary, patient
of suffering, kind to others, zealous for religion.
But let someone put out his hand and touch them
wrongfully, and the passion of resentment flares
up in their souls, and is not quenched; and the
Christian life which was so promising begins from
that day to decline until it falls to the ordinary
level we know so well. It is true that our Lord
spoke with more urgency on this topic than on
any other; it is also true that Christian experience
has abundantly justified all that urgency. The
difficulty of being forgiven is as nothing to the
difficulty of forgiving. Yet He has made "to be
forgiving" a necessary condition of "to be forgiven";
and He Himself cannot unmake it. The Kingdom
of Heaven is like this, essentially, unalterably.

X.

THE PARABLE OF THE LABOURERS

St. Matthew xx. 1-16.

For the kingdom of heaven is like unto a man that is an householder, which went out early in the morning to hire labourers into his vineyard. And when he had agreed with the labourers for a penny a day, he sent them into his vineyard. And he went out about the third hour, and saw others standing idle in the marketplace, and said unto them, Go ye also into the vineyard, and whatsoever is right I will give you. And they went their way. Again he went out about the sixth and ninth hour, and did likewise. And about the eleventh hour he went out, and found others standing idle, and saith unto them, Why stand ye here all the day idle? They say unto him, Because no man hath hired us. He saith unto them, Go ye also into the vineyard; and whatsoever is right, that shall ye receive. So when even was come, the lord of the vineyard saith unto his steward, Call the labourers, and give them their hire, beginning from the last unto the first. And when they came that were hired about the eleventh hour, they received every man a penny. But when the first came, they supposed that they should have received more; and they likewise received every man a penny. And when they had received it, they murmured against the goodman of the house, saying, These last have wrought but one hour, and thou hast made them equal unto us, which have borne the burden and heat of the day. But he answered one of them, and said, Friend, I do thee no wrong: didst not thou agree with me for a penny? Take that thine is, and go thy way: I will give unto this last, even as unto thee. Is it not lawful for me to do what I will with mine own? Is thine eye evil, because I am good? So the last shall be first, and the first last; for many be called, but few chosen.

IT is not altogether strange that it should have been St. Peter who drew from our Lord both this parable of the Kingdom and the last. For

good or evil he was always foremost, prompt to
act and quick to speak. The mistaken ideas which
he shared no doubt with the rest he was the only
one to put into words. He was but the spokesman
of the Twelve when he made his grand confession
at Cæsarea Philippi, and so he was no doubt when
he earned the frightful rebuke, "Get thee behind
Me, Satan." Like other people he was under
various misapprehensions about the characteristic
features of the Kingdom of Heaven; unlike them,
he expressed his errors in a crude sort of way, and
so gave our Lord the opportunity of setting him
(and all men) right.

What he had failed to understand on the previous
occasion had been this—that forgiving people is not
a matter of arithmetic, or of "limited liability" in
the Kingdom; it is a temper, essential and constant,
which only grows stronger as it is called into play.
What he failed to understand on this later occasion
was even more serious, for he completely mistook
the kind of temper with which a Christian must
regard the rewards of the Kingdom. And that
mistake was peculiarly unfortunate, because undoubtedly our Lord had a great deal to say about
those rewards. He had spoken of them without
reserve as far exceeding any earthly objects of
ambition. The rich young man who was asked
to give up all his earthly wealth was promised
"treasure in heaven" as more than compensation.
It would have been perfectly possible and natural
to apply the theory of "enlightened selfishness" to
our Lord's doctrine of the religious life, and in point

of fact St. Peter did understand Him in that sense. Rich men, he heard our Lord say, would have a tremendous difficulty in entering the Kingdom of Heaven—a difficulty amounting (humanly speaking) to a practical impossibility—because it is so hard to give up the substantial gratifications of the present (such as they are) for the vaguely-discerned rewards of the future. Without such renunciation these latter could not, of course, be had. Then St. Peter broke in with the question, "Lo, *we* have left all and followed Thee; what then shall *we* have?" What are *we* to get? An odious question, which betrayed so palpably the vulgarity of mind which made it possible! What are *we* to get—*we*, who have not gone sullenly away like yonder rich man; *we*, who left our nets and our business at Thy word? That is the genuine commercial spirit, which unconsciously exaggerates the little sacrifices it has made, which is eager to know what recompense it may reckon on. Implied, of course, was the contention that as they had given up more than others they were bound to get more in return. A million voices of Christian people throughout the world uttered themselves in St. Peter's words, "What then shall *we* have?"

It is wonderful to observe how our Lord responded to a demand so odious, in such bad taste, springing out of so much error. In His words (as we see), in His tones (as we may be sure), there was no severity, no reproof. It looked indeed at first sight as if He recognized and allowed that claim for exceptional payment (so to speak) for exceptional services. In the "regeneration" the Twelve should sit on thrones judging the twelve tribes of Israel. What a glow of satisfaction, of gratified ambition, must have come over St. Peter's mind as he heard that. Doubtless he himself, as the foremost of that devoted band, would occupy the highest throne and judge the tribe of Judah which God had chosen to be specially His own. Afterwards, in the light of later words and subsequent events, his thoughts will have been very different. In the "regeneration" there could be no possible place for any joy of pre-eminence, of mastery, of rule over others. Thrones would be no reward, and judging others no gratification. All such ambitions belong to this generation, and are bound to disappear in the regeneration. Then also it would occur to him that to have to judge the tribes of Israel would be as undesirable a business as could be conceived. Moses himself had found it a task beyond even his magnificent resources of strength and patience. Nothing in Israel's story is more wonderful or more sad than the way in which that great and faithful servant of God found himself thwarted, defeated, broken by the people whom he led out of Egypt. Not only did they die themselves, in spite of him, in the wilderness; they even made him share their sentence of exclusion from the Holy Land. Nothing more intractable could be conceived than the tribes of Israel, then and always; nothing more hopeless than the task of judging them. What was it then, this prize which looked so splendid? What did it mean? That devotion to the Master in this world, and renunciation of earthly prizes for His sake, shall lead on to far greater and more onerous responsibilities and duties and labours in the age to come. Simply that. There is no room in this promise (howsoever it may be fulfilled) for any expectation of pleasure, or satisfaction, or triumph; there is no prospect of anything but larger opportunity of spending and being spent in the service of others. This should be the reward of St. Peter, of the Twelve, and in proportion of all who had made real sacrifices for the Kingdom of Heaven's sake.

Then follows that parable of the Kingdom which has been so little understood in spite of the pains spent upon it. The motive of it has been too simple to be perceived amidst the laborious searchings of commentators and preachers. In the Kingdom of Heaven the commercial spirit, the temper which demands proportionate payment for efforts and sacrifices, has absolutely no place. That is all. As in so many other parables it is a temper which is inculcated (or rather it is a temper which is reprobated), it is not a transaction which is intimated. Read it as a transaction, in which God is concerned on the one hand and His ministering servants on the other, and we fall at once into difficulties out of which nothing can deliver us but the most arbitrary assumptions. It is not true, *e.g.*, that the reward which awaits the servants of God is in any real sense uniform—so that it may be fairly represented by the "penny" paid to each. That is against the whole drift of New Testament teaching, and it could not have been our Lord's intention

to teach it here. It is not true that the "penny"
would have been worth more to those who had
laboured long and hard to earn it. On the contrary
to these labourers, as to the average labourers everywhere, the extra toil was a cause of annoyance and
discontent. Still less is it any part of the parable
that work for such a Master is its own reward—is,
in fact, a privilege. These labourers would have
laughed any such notion to scorn, could they have
been got to understand it. Once more the householder's plea, that it was lawful for him to do what
he liked with his own, is untenable now—whatever
it was then. It belongs to a theory of property
which is still freely acted on, but already with a
certain shame. No really good man, employing
labour, would act now as this householder acted;
or, if he did, he would be held guilty of caprice
which could not be justified. When it came to the
turn of those first engaged he would say to them,
"I am not *legally* bound to give more to you than
to these last; but I think I ought to pay you more
for your extra work, and here it is." To suggest
that it can be "a righteous thing with God" to treat
His servants as a good landlord would be ashamed
to treat his labourers is useless. The fact is that
both householder and labourers in the parable are
no better and no worse than they were in real life.
He is capricious and unjust; they are greedy and
discontented. There is not anything in the Kingdom
of Heaven which corresponds to the very unsatisfactory transaction which forms the story of the
parable. It is the *temper*, the attitude of mind,

which the parable serves so admirably to bring home to us, which is alone important—profoundly important, because it has absolutely no place in the Kingdom. Like the unforgiving spirit, the commercial spirit is utterly banned, however naturally and with whatever excuses it may assert itself. There can be no rivalries, no jealousies, no clamours, no demands, "what then shall *we* have?" in the Kingdom. Doubtless it has its rewards, rewards quite freely spoken of by the Master and quite legitimately anticipated by the servant; but there is nothing commercial and nothing competitive about them.

As to the distribution of these rewards indeed, there are two things certain. Nothing done for the Master will be *unrewarded*, not even a cup of cold water given to a disciple, much less the heroic sacrifices of heroic souls; nothing will fail to be recompensed beyond all desiring or deserving; of which great promise there be many startling foretastes even in this world. Again, there is nothing whatever said or known as to how the rewards distributed will compare with one another. If anyone asks, "what then shall *I* have?" the book is shut in his face, and he only hears that "the last shall be first, and the first last"; in other words it is the unexpected that will happen. In this world we are doomed to live under the *régime* of competition. We may hate it, but we have to resign ourselves to it, and console ourselves with thinking that a law so deeply impressed upon nature must on the whole be good. But it has no place in the

Kingdom of Heaven, and this parable was designed to force that fact upon us in a way very much more picturesque and therefore more permanently telling than any other which could have been adopted.

XI

THE TWO PARABLES OF THE VINEYARD

St. Matthew xxi. 28–32; 33–43.

But what think ye? A certain man had two sons; and he came to the first, and said, Son, go work to-day in my vineyard. He answered and said, I will not: but afterward he repented, and went. And he came to the second, and said likewise. And he answered and said, I go, sir; and went not. Whether of them twain did the will of his father? They say unto him, The first. Jesus saith unto them, Verily I say unto you, That the publicans and the harlots go into the kingdom of God before you. For John came unto you in the way of righteousness, and ye believed him not; but the publicans and the harlots believed him; and ye, when ye had seen it, repented not afterward, that ye might believe him.

Hear another parable: There was a certain householder, which planted a vineyard, and hedged it round about, and digged a winepress in it, and built a tower, and let it out to husbandmen, and went into a far country: And when the time of the fruit drew near, he sent his servants to the husbandmen, that they might receive the fruits of it. And the husbandmen took his servants, and beat one, and killed another, and stoned another. Again, he sent other servants more than the first; and they did unto them likewise. But last of all he sent unto them his son, saying, They will reverence my son. But when the husbandmen saw the son, they said among themselves, This is the heir; come, let us kill him, and let us seize on his inheritance. And they caught him, and cast him out of the vineyard, and slew him. When the lord therefore of the vineyard cometh, what will he do unto those husbandmen? They say unto him, He will miserably destroy those wicked men, and will let out his vineyard unto other husbandmen, which shall render him the fruits in their seasons. Jesus saith

unto them, Did ye never read in the scriptures, The stone which
the builders rejected, the same is become the head of the corner : this
is the Lord's doing, and it is marvellous in our eyes ?   Therefore say I
unto you, The kingdom of God shall be taken from you, and given to
a nation bringing forth the fruits thereof.

IN St. Matthew xxi. there are two parables—of the
two sons, and of the wicked husbandmen—which
are somewhat less definitely parables of the Kingdom
than the others in our list. They do not begin with
the formula, " The Kingdom of Heaven is like unto,"
and in the application of them our Lord speaks
of " the Kingdom of *God.*" But this (though unusual in the first Gospel) is not discernibly different
from the more familiar phrase, and its employment
warrants us in claiming these parables also for our
present purpose. They differ widely in scope from
most of the others, and are all the more valuable for
that reason. The story of the two sons is too short,
and in its moral too obvious, to be in itself instructive. No one, however stupid or prejudiced, could
hesitate to answer, " The first," when asked which
of the two was the better son. A rude manner and
unpromising appearance is always a less evil than
disobedience and deceit. It is in the application of it
made by our Lord to the various classes of society in
Israel that the interest lies. The publicans and
harlots, He said — *i.e.*, the disreputable people
generally—were more likely to find their way into
the Kingdom than the chief priests and elders of the
people. We are not surprised at that. The great
parable of the Pharisee and the Publican has made
the idea very familiar to us. It is clear that our

Lord felt and spoke of the class which was not respectable—which formed the " Bohemia " of His day—as if it were on the whole more hopeful than the strictly religious class. Underneath their irreligion and their vice He recognized in many of them an "honest and good heart," which would respond to His teaching when it got a chance. He saw also that they had more readiness to take a line of their own, and were less under the evil bondage of the example and opinion of their fellows than those who belonged to the religious world. Most of all, He knew that a disreputable life is a less fatal hindrance to self-knowledge and self-renunciation than pride and hardness and the habit of looking down upon others. Therefore His relations with the Bohemia of His day were sufficiently friendly to scandalize even those who wished Him well. They were, perhaps, quite genuinely sorry to hear of that supper in the house of Levi the publican, where our Lord was mixed up with a crowd of people, male and female, whose antecedents were worse than doubtful and whose characters were very shady. It was indeed impossible that He could have felt at home with them. Yet He was better pleased there than at the table of Simon the Pharisee, because the barrier which separated Him from them was far less hopeless. In point of fact many a publican left his odious gains, and many a harlot left her sinful life, at His call. We do not know that any Scribe or Pharisee left his self-esteem and self-importance at His word. Such is human nature, that the vices which are esteemed (and justly) to be lower and more disgraceful often leave untouched the capacity for moral heroism and for generous self-sacrifice : whereas nothing is so fatal to this capacity as the selfish habit of mind which often goes along with an extreme and studied respectability of life. It is quite notorious that the men—and women too, when they get a chance—who do splendid things for others, are more likely to be horrid blackguards than to have a reputation for piety. Chivalry, generosity of soul, a certain recklessness in seizing upon some high ideal and following it even unto death—these virtues do flourish in Bohemia, unchoked by the vices which we should have expected to destroy them. Now it is precisely these virtues which get people into the Kingdom of Heaven, in our Lord's way of looking at it. "The Kingdom of Heaven suffereth violence, and the violent take it by force "— take it by storm, as we should say now. What is wanted is a certain recklessness which does not count the cost, which cares nothing what other people will say, which scarcely stops to think what it involves ; and this happy recklessness is extremely rare in people of carefully-ordered lives.

It seems absolutely necessary that we should have our eyes open to this fact about the Kingdom, because it enables us to estimate at its fair value a great part of the moral teaching of modern fiction. Much of that fiction has of course no moral teaching, and does not pretend to. But where it has, it commonly takes the line of glorifying the disreputable side of society, or at least of showing how much of what is admirable may be found in the most reckless and deliberate of sinners. Mixed with much petulant (and perhaps self-interested) revolt against the ordinary moral standards of Christianity, there is an honest and righteous recognition of the truth so often and so strongly asserted by our Lord. The mere fact of being conformed to the moral standards of the day does involve two very serious dangers. The more obvious of the two (and therefore the less dangerous) is that of self-satisfaction, of censoriousness, of despising others. The more subtle and more commonly fatal is that of conventionality. The Kingdom of Heaven makes its most characteristic appeal to the chivalrous instincts, the heroic impulses, the latent capacities for a splendid self-devotion, which are the very best things in our nature. But the very fact of being conformed to moral standards gives those standards, and the general body of average opinion by which they are supported, a tremendous power over us. They tend to restrain us as much from rising above them as from falling beneath them. That which should only support us at a certain level also keeps us at that level. The instincts and impulses of our nature, habitually checked when they make for evil, are similarly hampered when they make for good. It will always be true then that "Bohemia" will stand in some ways more closely related to the Kingdom of Heaven than the "religious world": and to this extent the moral teaching of modern fiction is justified. But beyond pointing out and dwelling upon this fact (for which we are indebted to it), modern fiction has no message, no Gospel. It cannot seriously desire its readers to become publicans and harlots in order to attain to their freedom from the dreadful trammels of conventionality: and it has not anything else to propose. It is, alas, beyond its purpose or its power to declare that "conventionality" in religion (or even in morals) is excluded and condemned by almost every word our Lord uttered: that the "enlightened selfishness" which is the dominant motive of the religious world is the precise opposite of what He taught: that the appeal to what is chivalrous and disinterested in men, although it may be latent, is only latent in Christianity because it has been wilfully obscured. Take two lives, familiar enough to us—the life of a respectable churchgoer on the one hand, who desires to "make the best of both worlds," and the life of some disreputable creature on the other. In the eyes of men these lives are divided by a great gulf. In the eyes of Christ they are equally unsatisfactory, although there are elements of hopefulness about both. That life is the more hopeful of the two which is the more likely to catch the infection of a real and true and unselfish enthusiasm for Him and for His service.

The second of these two parables of the vineyard is once more astonishingly different in its scope, and has to be classed with the parables of the mustard seed and of the drag-net as dealing with the Kingdom in its outward and visible aspect. For the vineyard of St. Matthew xxi. 33–43, is for all practical purposes the Church. "The Kingdom of God shall be taken away from you and shall be given to a nation bringing forth the fruits thereof."

What is that but a prophecy that the visible Society which in past history had been Jewish should in future history be Christian? The vineyard with its fence and winepress and tower is here, as in Isaiah v., the Church of God with its separate character, its peculiar institutions, its various arrangements for the promotion of holy living. It had been the property of the Jews—their private and inalienable property as they fancied—only theirs on lease and on conditions as God continually warned them. And now the end was come, and it was about to be transferred to another "nation." This is remarkable, because it puts in the most emphatic way an aspect of the Kingdom which even St. Paul, Apostle of the Gentiles as he was, scarcely seemed to realize. For him the Church always seemed to have a double character, Jewish and Gentile, the two walls which found their common corner-stone in Christ. Here the transfer is absolute and the distinction sharp and final. And so, of course, it was in effect. The Jewish remnant which believed had no lasting influence. The community of Israel re-formed itself after the destruction of Jerusalem, and lived on outside the Church of God, having lost the vineyard for ever. And the Christian Church which *had*, or rather *was*, the vineyard, was for all intents and purposes a Gentile Church. What even the Apostles did not altogether foresee (unless it were St. John at Ephesus) came to pass, according to the word of Christ. Thus we have established, upon a basis which cannot be shaken, the historical continuity between the Church of the old dispensation and that of the new. The institution itself—the Kingdom of God, as a thing taking visible shape under human conditions—abides, indestructible. Only it is transferred from one set of "occupiers" to another. To the Jews succeed the Christians as the chosen people of God, and these Christians are "a nation." However much recruited out of "every nation," however representative of "all tribes and peoples and tongues," they are in our Lord's view of them sufficiently distinct and sufficiently homogeneous to be called a nation. It is necessary to remember this in an age when there seems to be so little to hold Christendom together, and when the Kingdom of Heaven might be judged to have no definite boundaries and no recognizable feature common to all its members. Over against the Jews, with their so sharply defined and jealously limited nationality, the Christians are also "a nation." That is only one aspect of the Kingdom out of many. But it must not be ignored. The Church exists for the purpose of yielding the fruits of righteousness : it is a Society of holy living ; but it is not the less a Society, a Church, a Nation.

XII.

THE PARABLE OF THE KING'S SUPPER

THE PARABLE OF THE WEDDING AND OF THE WEDDING GUEST

St. Matthew xxii. 2–14.

The kingdom of heaven is like unto a certain king, which made a marriage for his son, and sent forth his servants to call them that were bidden to the wedding : and they would not come. Again, he sent forth other servants, saying, Tell them which are bidden, Behold, I have prepared my dinner : my oxen and my fatlings are killed, and all things are ready : come unto the marriage. But they made light of it, and went their ways, one to his farm, another to his merchandise : and the remnant took his servants, and entreated them spitefully, and slew them. But when the king heard thereof, he was wroth : and he sent forth his armies, and destroyed those murderers, and burned up their city. Then saith he to his servants, The wedding is ready, but they which were bidden were not worthy. Go ye therefore into the highways, and as many as ye shall find, bid to the marriage. So those servants went out into the highways, and gathered together all as many as they found, both bad and good : and the wedding was furnished with guests.

And when the king came in to see the guests, he saw there a man which had not on a wedding garment : and he saith unto him, Friend, how camest thou in hither not having a wedding garment? And he was speechless. Then said the king to the servants, Bind him hand and foot, and take him away, and cast him into outer darkness ; there shall be weeping and gnashing of teeth. For many are called, but few are chosen.

THIS parable may fairly be said to be the gloomiest ever spoken by our Lord. It is almost savage in its twofold severity. Spoken to Jews, and dealing primarily with their apostacy

(which is represented as total and irremediable), it
goes on to crush by an awful example the least
tendency to exultation on the part of Christians.
Following closely upon the last, and dealing with
the Kingdom from the same general point of view
(as first rejected by the Jews and then bestowed
upon the Christians), it is nevertheless very much
more disquieting as regards the latter. It may be
supposed that our Lord either perceived or foresaw
among His followers a certain tendency to rest
content with the outward calling and character of a
Christian, as though that were in itself sufficient
safeguard against the wrath to come. So He
seems to have repeated with some variety of detail
a parable which He had made use of at least
once before (St. Luke xiv.), and to have added
to it that incident of the wedding guest which
forms by far the most remarkable feature of the
story as it stands here. That this incident formed
no part of the original parable is evident from its
incongruity. It introduces considerations of an
entirely different character, and emphasizes an
aspect of the Kingdom which is remote from the
one with which the parable as a whole is concerned.
It reminds us of that part of the story of Dives and
Lazarus about the brethren of Dives, which it is so
impossible to bring into any connection with the
rest. That also may be looked upon as an addition
to the story as originally told, an addition which our
Lord made in order to meet some pressing need,
although it undoubtedly impaired the dramatic
power of that amazing narrative.

In the present case our Lord was evidently concerned to draw His picture of the Kingdom in the darkest possible colours. It may be that in that hour His soul also "was filled with the scornful reproof of the wealthy, and with the despitefulness of the proud."[1]   On the one hand the Jews weighed upon His mind, and on the other Judas, until His soul was "exceeding sorrowful even unto death." So He deliberately darkened the already dark colours in which He had painted the rejection of His invitations by the Jews, and their subsequent fate.   Them He made to be murderers, as well as scorners, and their destiny to be destruction as well as exclusion.   He spoke not obscurely of the cruel persecution which they would raise against His disciples, and of the vengeance which would fall upon their nation and city.   Having done this, and having intimated that the places which they left empty would all the same be filled, He then turned upon these other guests thus graciously invited and admitted, and bade them see what *they* might expect if they presumed upon His goodness.   Certainly our Lord never used in His teaching any piece of imagery more frightful than this of the man without a wedding garment.   The horribleness of it might really be considered gratuitous if it were not His. The wretched man had not asked to come to that feast.   He had been gathered in with a miscellaneous crowd (" both bad and good ") by the king's servants. He had to come in as he was, presumably.   The king's orders left no room for enquiry as to whether

---

[1] Psalm cxxiii. 4, P.B. Version.

he possessed a wedding garment or no. The action of the king indeed in this matter is, on the face of it, arbitrary and passionate. There may have been a great number of these ill-assorted guests in the like predicament. But this one happens to catch his eye, and to offend his mind, and so he orders him to be cruelly punished. Now of course it is true here, as elsewhere, that our Lord takes no pains to draw men better than they really are. Kings — in popular imagination at any rate — are not troubled with any scruples. They have their generous impulses, and like to fill their palaces with guests. But if they are insulted or aggrieved their vengeance knows no pity, and their anger no moderation. So it is here. The "certain king" does not represent the Father of Heaven except for the particular purpose of the parable; nor does the parable itself represent more than one particular aspect (presumably a very limited one) of the Kingdom.

But making the fullest allowance for this, the alternative suggested, and meant to be suggested, by the parable is really frightful. Either you are to be excluded from the Kingdom altogether, or you become liable to an investigation which you cannot stand, and a punishment which you dare not contemplate. If you refuse to enter you will be destroyed; if you venture to enter you run the chance of being cast out into outer darkness. Nor is this suggestion really mitigated by the commonly-received explanation that every guest so invited received the offer of a suitable garment as he went

in. That *may* have been the case at royal enter-
tainments of such a character; but it looks much
more like one of those ingenious devices for turning
the edge of a hard saying (like the "needle's-eye"
gate at Hebron),[1] which we have learnt to regard
with so much suspicion. At any rate, although it
may be lawful to introduce this explanation for
certain purposes of teaching, it is clear that we have
no right to read it into the parable. If our Lord's
point had really been that the unhappy man was
without a wedding garment *because he had refused
to put one on*, He would have said so. This
habit of reading things into parables because they
have to be made to square with our own precon-
ceived view of their meaning is utterly indefensible.
The fact is simply that the affair *as our Lord
related it* has no moral character. It is the act of
an irresponsible tyrant which may, or may not,
be justified by something which he knows about
the object of his wrath. But whether he is thus
justified is not in question at all. It does not fall
to be considered. The only matter which concerns
us is that the man was thus treated because he did
not have on a wedding garment. There is a danger,
a very real and pressing danger, corresponding to
this in the Kingdom of Heaven — a danger which
arises out of the peculiar conditions which govern
admission into that Kingdom. For beyond doubt
(as we have certainly gathered from other parables)
the conditions of admission have but little connection
with moral fitness. The sweep of the net includes

[1] See Mr. WRIGHT's *Some New Testament Problems*, pp. 125 ff.

those "of every kind," and it is only at the end
that the bad are cast away. So here "the servants
gathered together all as many as they found, both
bad and good." The membership of the Church
has always been more or less indiscriminate. No
human wisdom or effort will make it otherwise. No
doubt the message appeals most to the best, but
it is impossible to prevent its being attractive to
many who are deceived and some who are deceivers.
Simon Magus also was baptized—and it has not
been suggested that Philip was unduly lax or
culpably careless. There is no missionary, at all
successful, who does not admit "converts" who are
morally unsound and spiritually unfit. And when
it comes to the children of converts (whether infant
or adult) then the sweep of the net becomes
practically undistinguishing. The majority, who
have but little religion or irreligion of their own,
will always want to follow the religion of their
fathers, and will always persuade themselves that
they too believe it. It cannot be helped, and
moreover it is the Lord's will. But then it involves
a frightful danger. The moral side of the Kingdom
cannot be set aside because admission to the
Kingdom is free, and in a certain sense indiscriminate. How it is to be worked out no man
really knows, because all that is told us is by way
of illustrating principles, not by way of describing
events.

But the danger to the individual is of the
most pressing and terrible character, and therefore
our Lord seeks to bring it home by this frightful

example. "You are Christians," He says in effect, "and the Kingdom of Heaven is yours now. It has been taken from the Jews and given to you. The places reserved for them of old at the Marriage Supper of the Lamb have been thrown open to you, and you have filled them. Blessed are they which are bidden to that Supper. Blessed indeed, if they be found worthy, so that they may walk with Him in white, and sit down with Him at His table. But cursed are they, and all the more cursed, if they are found unworthy; it were better for them not to have known the way of righteousness. Therefore be not high-minded, but fear." That is what He says in this parable; and the very gloom of it, the sense of darkness and despondency which clings to it, makes the warning all the more emphatic.

When we consider in how many lands and under how many circumstances Christian people rejoice in their Christianity, and yet show no appreciable conformity to Christ, we perceive that the gloom of the parable is not inexplicable nor its harshness out of keeping. If any man enquire concerning the garment, by what standard of beauty or expensiveness it shall be judged whether it can be passed as a wedding garment or no, he shall get no information here. Only it would seem, *that* theory is false which is widely held, that every Christian will be "saved" who does not apostatize but clings to his Christian profession to the end and accepts the outward rites belonging to it. That is to say every guest who has been let in, and who does not vacate his place, will be suffered to remain. The parable does not square with any such teaching. Its terrors are (it may be) vague, but they are hopelessly inconsistent with that kind of religious optimism.

XIII

THE THREE PARABLES OF ST. MATTHEW XXV.

IT may be assumed that this wonderful group of parables, which has exercised such an extraordinary influence over the minds of Christians in all generations, has a unity of its own—a subordinate unity indeed, since for certain purposes these parables may easily be co-ordinated with others—but still a unity which is sufficiently striking. They have in common a sense of being dominated by the Presence of our Lord Himself, and again, of being closely connected with His second coming, which are nothing like so clearly marked elsewhere. No one doubts that the Bridegroom of the first, and the Lord of the second, is as much our Saviour as the King of the third parable ; and it is our Saviour in the Regeneration when He shall have come "in His Kingdom," as the dying robber expressed it. They are not indeed parables of the Second Advent in the sense in which they have been popularly understood, but on the face of them they are clearly enough bound up with what our Lord taught towards the end of His ministry about His coming again. It will be necessary, therefore, in order to understand them aright, to investigate at some little length what that teaching really came to. To examine this subject thoroughly it would be necessary to follow out in its slow development the doctrine of the Old Testament concerning the Future. The more we did so the more clearly it would appear that there is a real continuity between that doctrine and our Lord's, which is of the utmost importance for the interpretation of the latter. We must be content here to indicate the lines of agreement very briefly. It is, of course, known to all thoughtful readers that there is no trace of a future life in the Law of Moses. Revealed religion was absolutely concentrated upon the present life, upon the worship and service of God, upon the enjoyment of God's favour and presence, here and now. The problems of the future, of what lies beyond the grave, were left severely alone. It is certain that men must have speculated, more or less eagerly, about these problems in Israel, as they did in Egypt; but these speculations, though not prohibited, received no encouragement. No light reached them but that which was reflected from the revealed goodness and faithfulness of God *now and here.* Gradually, very gradually, men came to feel with a certain assurance that God could not cease to be their God, could not become less their God, because they died. It is precisely this feeling, and nothing else, which gave force and life to our Lord's argument from the words, " I am the God of Abraham, and the God of Isaac, and the God of Jacob."[1] As an argument from *words* it is nought. As an argument from the character of God it is

---

[1] Mark xii. 26,

everything. Since He is still willing to be known as the God of Abraham, it is certain He cannot have allowed His "friend" to lapse into nothingness. Abraham must still live, and must some day be restored to the perfectness of human life in body as well as soul. Long before our Lord's day this conviction had so far prevailed that in the Book of Job, and in a few of the Psalms, and in one or two places of the Prophets, we find anticipations and assurances, few and brief and for the most part vague, of immortal life and the resurrection of the body. In Daniel xii. 2 we find for the first time the thought of retribution distinctly connected with the resurrection. If God's goodness must recall His friends to joy and blessedness, His justice must also recall His enemies to suffer the due reward of their deeds. These convictions rapidly spread and expanded in the age when our Lord came, and a large apocalyptic literature sprang up (which passed over into Christian circles) describing in a crude and materialistic way the events of the last day, the rewards of the saved and the torments of the lost.

In His own teaching our Lord distinctly adopted and enforced the Old Testament standpoint that the true centre of Life is here and now. It is of the first importance to realize that our Lord's doctrine was essentially that of the Prophets and Psalmists of Israel in this matter, in spite of all apparent differences. Life eternal is a *present* possession which He came at once to reveal and to impart. It may be said with equal truth to stand in the *knowledge* of God and of Christ, or in active *obedience*, or in an inner *fellow-*

ship; but anyhow, Life eternal must be had here and
now in order to be had at all. Against this Life what
we call death (what our Saviour would only allow to
be *sleep*) has no power. This powerlessness He used
to express in such paradoxical sayings as " He that
believeth in Me shall live though he die; and he that
liveth and believeth in Me shall never die."[1] He ob-
literates death, as it were, for His own, and while He
does not of course mean to deny the mere physical
fact, He treats it as a negligible quantity, as a thing
which from His point of view may be ignored, since it
has no fundamental significance. At bottom therefore
our Lord's attitude towards death is the very same
as that of the Psalmist and Prophet, in spite of the
superficial difference which is so striking. Both
ignored death in speaking of the essential relationship of the soul to God. The Psalmist ignored it,
because he knew nothing of what it meant, and had
only a vague and desperate hope which he hardly
dared to express, that it would not separate him
from God. Our Lord ignored it because He knew
it would make no real difference. In either case
the life in God now and here is the one important
thing. And this is without doubt the most distinctively Christian attitude towards death and that which
comes after. " Do not trouble about these things,"
our Lord says in effect, " do not mind. Concentrate
yourself upon to-day. Live for God, live in God,
to-day. Enjoy to the full that fellowship which
He offers you to-day. Never mind to-morrow : that
will be all right. Never mind the eternal morrow :

[1] John xi. 25, 26.

that will be all right too, for God will take care of
it." No one can well deny that such *is* the general
effect of our Lord's teaching about Life eternal. It
is a teaching which makes everything turn upon the
present, and wholly discourages that rather futile
"futuristic" temper which has been so characteristic
of popular Christianity. Probably the tone of mind
which is reflected in the lines "There is a happy land,
far, far away," and in so many hymns sung by older
people, has done more to enfeeble and sterilize the
Christianity of the masses than anything else. The
centre of gravity is shifted from the present (where
it ought always to be) into the more or less dreamy
and visionary future, where it ought emphatically *not*
to be. It is not only "hell" that has been preached
to the miserable lowering of the whole tone of religion among Christians : it is quite as much Heaven.
We have, for the most part, fallen far below the
spiritual level of the Hebrew Psalmist, who for the
love he had towards God and for the joy he felt in
His favour and fellowship was content *not* to think
what would happen when inevitable death came his
way. We, alas, are almost content to live without
God to-day, because we expect to enjoy Him on
some distant shore "far, far away."

But while our Lord laid the greatest stress upon
the fact that Eternal Life is here and now, and is
merely continued without interruption past the bars
of death, it is yet certain that He *did* teach a doctrine
of things to come. He taught it mainly, as would
appear, to His chosen disciples, but that makes little
difference. We have to take it into account, at any

rate in certain broad aspects of it. If it be impossible to give any really satisfactory explanation of it, we shall at least be able to see where popular notions about it are untenable.

Now the first thing that must inevitably strike us is that our Lord's doctrine of things to come is wholly connected with His own Coming. The ideas which are so familiar to us from the three parables of St. Matthew xxv. are expressed in a less dramatic form in almost all other places where He speaks of the end of the world. But this Coming of His, round which all the crucial events of the future revolve, He uniformly represents as being close at hand : practically, within the lifetime of those then present. " Verily I say unto you, this generation shall not pass away, till all these things be accomplished. Heaven and earth shall pass away, but My words shall not pass away."[1] It is possible no doubt to explain the word " generation " in a figurative sense so as to include all Christians, as members of one family. But no one who heard Him could possibly have understood Him so, and that seems sufficient answer. It is true also that He went on to declare His own ignorance of the " day " or the " hour," *i.e.* of the precise date. But here again those who listened to Him must inevitably have understood that while the precise date was not revealed even to Him, yet the approximate date (within the next forty years, let us say) *was* known to Him. Nor can any of the commonly-urged explanations touch that other saying, " Verily I say unto you, Ye shall not have gone

[1] Matt. xxiv. 34.

through the cities of Israel, till the Son of man be come."[1]   Even if sufficient ingenuity could succeed in neutralizing the effect of these and other sayings taken separately, yet the combined effect of all of them together would remain overwhelming.   There is no real question that the only natural way, and therefore the only reverent way, of understanding them is the way in which they actually were understood.   Our Lord's teaching about His second Coming as received by St. Paul, and as reproduced by him at Thessalonica in the earlier years of his ministry, had an unmistakable effect.   The Thessalonians were so persuaded that the Lord was to come quickly, even in their lifetime, that when some of their number died they were greatly disturbed about them, as though they had lost their share in the glories of that glorious day.   St. Paul had to explain to them that the dead in Christ would not be any worse off than " we that are alive, that are left unto the coming of the Lord."[2]   No doubt, as years went on, the keenness of the expectation somewhat diminished, and practical exigencies led the Apostles to dwell rather upon other topics.   Yet such expressions as those of St. James, " the Judge standeth before the doors,"[3] " The coming of the Lord is at hand,"[4] and those of St. Peter, " The end of all things is at hand,"[5] " Looking for and earnestly desiring the coming of the day of God,"[6] abundantly testify to the apostolic belief that their Master would

[1] Matt. x. 23.
[2] 1 Thess. iv. 15.
[3] James v. 9.
[4] *Ibid.* 8.
[5] 1 Peter iv. 7.
[6] 2 Peter iii. 12.

come again very shortly indeed. It is not necessary to give any explanation of this fact. Whether we like it or not it is a fact, and a fact of primary importance in considering our Lord's teaching about the last things. The Apostles did not use such language about the Lord's coming *because it was the conventional language of the Church* (as perhaps we do), but because they understood Him in that sense. And they only did what we ourselves should have done. He so worded His prophetic utterances about the eternal future, He threw His parables of the last things into such a shape, and gave them such a colouring, that men inevitably expected Him to return and to bring "eternity" with Him in their own lifetime. In His prophecies and parables death was left out : there was no room for death, no time to die, except as an exceptional thing for which special provision would be made. In point of fact when Christian people began to die in any numbers (as at Thessalonica) Christian teaching about the future had to be modified, reconsidered, supplemented (however we like to phrase it), in order to meet a state of things which had not been contemplated. As in the spiritual teaching of St. John's Gospel, so also in the eschatology of the Synoptists (but after an entirely independent fashion), death is ignored or treated as a "negligible quantity." That is a note of unity underlying difference which is worth remembering.

The effect then of our Lord's teaching about His own Return was to bring the Eternal Future into the very closest relation to the present. Life and death,

Heaven and hell, are not relegated (as in popular
religious teaching) to a misty and far off future:
they spring immediately and directly out of *to-day*,
with no great gulf between. To-day you have to
see that you have oil in your lamps; to-day you
have to turn the Master's talents to best account;
to-day you have to relieve the Master's wants and
woes in the persons of His brothers and sisters;
because to-morrow He will be here, and give you
your portion accordingly. It is indeed hardly a
doctrine of the future at all, because that future is
so close and so direct. The Judge is at the door;
His finger is on the latch; the next word you speak,
the next thing you do, may be the last before the
"Eternal Future" has begun for you. That is the
effect of our Lord's teaching, and it must have been
intentional.

Now how is this affected by the obvious fact that
our Lord has not yet come again? There cannot
possibly be a question more important or more
urgently needing some sort of answer. On the
face of it (we need not hesitate to say) our Lord's
anticipations of speedy return have been falsified
by the event. What must we conclude from that
fact? Common sense must at any rate draw *one*
conclusion; and would invariably do so if it were
not stifled oftentimes by a wholly irreligious dread
of looking facts in the face. The only natural and
obvious *time* indication in the New Testament prophecies of the Second Advent has turned out to be
entirely delusive. There is really no question as to
that. What follows? Why, for anyone that has not

abjured his common sense in these matters, it follows without a shadow of a doubt that all speculations about the future based upon prophecies or parables of the New Testament are not worth the paper they are written upon. Scripture itself lets us know, in the most striking fashion, that the most ancient and obvious of all calculations about the Coming of Christ, although made by Apostles and made from the Master's own words, turned out to be a mistake (chronologically speaking). It is absolutely impossible that any other calculation of times and seasons can have one-hundredth part as much to say for itself as that which prevailed among the earliest Christians—and was utterly wrong. To ask any man to whom God has been pleased to continue the light of reason to consider the grounds of these calculations is an affront. It is an affront to one's piety as well as to one's common sense. It has pleased God that the only natural and obvious interpretation of our Lord's own words about His Return should be falsified by the event. Whatever else that was meant to teach us, it was certainly meant to make us not merely sceptical of, but absolutely indifferent to, any other speculation whatever which attempts to lay down any time limits for that Return. Anyone who pays heed to such speculations is simply besotted, and can only be treated as one whom God has given over to a spirit of delusion, because he has rejected the plain teaching of His Holy Word.

This lesson, however, is only a negative one, and therefore can only hold a secondary place in the Divine purpose. The other and greater truth remains.

Our Lord spoke constantly of His Second Coming so as to make us feel that the Kingdom of Heaven is continuous, is both immanent and imminent; that the present and the future run into one another without a break, that death is of little or no account, that life is made up of "to-days," and that on each "to-day" hang all the issues of eternity. It is clear enough that the simplest and directest way to create this kind of spiritual atmosphere was to speak as if His return was to be immediate—within the lifetime of those who heard Him. That He did so speak is certain, unless we are to discard the Gospel records wholesale, confirmed as these are by the evident belief of the first disciples. *How* He could so speak, when He was not to fulfil that expectation in fact, is a difficulty which we cannot possibly avoid. We may think that it can be explained in perfect conformity with the conditions under which the Incarnate Son of God was manifested for our salvation. Or we may have to confess that for us the difficulty is insoluble at present. But at any rate He *did* so speak, and at any rate we can see that it was the best thing possible for the Kingdom of God, not for the time being merely, but for all time. The apparent failure of the prediction made, has brought into stronger relief the spiritual truth inculcated. It does not matter now, not the very least, whether the Second Advent be delayed a million million years. That is indeed very possible, since there are really no reasons whatever for supposing it nearer—no reasons at all which did not already exist (in greater force perhaps) many many centuries ago. It does not make any difference, because mere lapse of time is clearly not a factor at all in matters of eternal concern. For all Christians it remains for ever true, above all things true, that we have to live in God and for God *to-day*, exactly as if to-day were destined to run on without a break into the eternal future. The great thing is that nothing really *intervenes* between us and His Coming. Death does not, for death makes no difference. Time does not, for time cannot alter anything in our relations to Him. The principle of religion which underlies all our Lord's references to His Second Coming is just this, that His Return is *the next thing* for all of us at all times. Straight out of to-day we are to look across the unknown gulfs of time into the glory and the terror of that Day. That is the Christian temper, by which all that is serious, and strenuous, and arduous, in the Christian life is regulated and sustained. Shall we be surprised if we discover that, in His prophecies as well as in His parables, our Lord *did not so much intimate an occurrence as inculcate a temper?* It is certain that this was very largely the case with the Prophets of old.

The same great principle must explain our Lord's absolute reticence about the intermediate state—the state of the departed between death and judgment. As He ignored death so He ignored what comes after death. For Him (and mostly for His apostles) death is out of sight. There is not any time allowed in the Kingdom of Heaven for people to *die*. What lies before the disciple is the Second Coming of the Lord, and the searching glance of His eye, and the praise or blame which fall from His lips. Blessed is

that servant whom the Lord when He cometh shall
find watching. That is the key-note. Of course
some *do* die. Some saints "slept" even when Christ
was upon earth. Yet it may be thought that these
were raised either by our Lord during His ministry,
or at His resurrection. Anyhow theirs is not the
normal case (if we may say so) and is almost dis-
regarded. St. Paul had to supply the Thessalonians
with special information about *them*—information, be
it noted, which concerned itself exclusively with what
would happen when Christ came. There is an almost
unbroken silence in the New Testament about the
state of the departed between death and judgment—
a silence which has afforded large scope, but very
little countenance, to a multitude of speculations.
Nothing throws the silence of Scripture into stronger
relief than the desperate shifts to which men are
reduced in order to find something to assert about
the intermediate state. Our Lord told a story—a
most vividly dramatic story—about the rich man and
Lazarus, and how they fared before and after their
decease. The story is designedly clothed in the
crudely materialistic language current among the
Jews, because it is directed against Jewish covetousness and Jewish superstition. God is not referred to
in the story. Father Abraham is the "divinity" of
the piece. No Christian can by any possibility accept
the theology which is implied in it—because it is
simply the theology of a debased Judaism which
looked no higher than to "Father Abraham" for
hope of good things in the life to come. It is in the
highest degree irrational and irreverent to reject (as

all Christians do) the materialistic details of the story, and yet to draw deductions—as that people will recognize one another in the intermediate state—from the very details rejected. We can learn nothing, because we were intended to learn nothing, from the story save what our Lord designed to teach; the utter hollowness of those words "rich" and "poor" as commonly used; and the utter uselessness of Father Abraham or any other such friend and patron to alter our fate in the world to come. Others again have sought to found a doctrine of purgatory upon St. Paul's language in 1 Corinthians iii. It is absolutely clear that when St. Paul speaks of "the day" testing every man's work "because it is revealed in fire," he is talking (as usual) about our Lord's Coming, and how He will show everybody and everything up exactly as they really are—a process in which a multitude of unfounded reputations and an enormous mass of misdirected and self-ended activities will perish like leaves and stubble in the flame.

There is in fact *no* doctrine of the intermediate state in the New Testament. There is simply the assurance that the servants of Christ will be "with Christ" in some very happy sense; but where, or how, or under what conditions we know not at all. There is also the general conviction that He who hath begun a good work in us will go on with it after death as well as before. Beyond this there is nothing but speculation. Reason, when it has to consider the actual state of those that die, demands that there shall be some provision made for their purification.

Piety itself can hardly help believing that the easy-going Christian, who has wasted most of his life and never realized his responsibilities, will not see the Lord without also seeing himself and suffering an unspeakable agony of shame and sorrow. But the doctrine of Purgatory, albeit that it seems to find as much favour to-day with Nonconformists as with Romanists, is a speculation founded entirely on certain conclusions of reason and piety. It may, or may not, be true; but it has not a word of Scripture to base itself upon. Our Lord has *no* doctrine of the intermediate life, because it is His practice ever to ignore death, and what lies beyond, and to direct our gaze right across and above the gulfs of time upon the distant hills which stand out so clear and sharp in the light of His Second Coming. Thirty years ago a certain doctrine of the inter-mediate state was taught with much confidence in Anglican circles. To-day it is scorned and flouted by not a few who are counted as authorities, and another doctrine quite different is taught instead. It is not to be wondered at: the one is as wanting in any real authority as the other. No books which deal with the state of the departed are of the slightest value, from whatever quarter they come. That those who die in the Lord are blessed we all know; [1] and there is nothing else that we can know.

What we come to then is this. There is in the New Testament a doctrine of future things which seems in some ways to be curiously imperfect, in other ways has the appearance of being very definite

[1] Rev. xiv. 13.

and precise. It has commonly been taught to
Christians as very definite and precise in these latter
ways. But the moment we begin to examine this
doctrine with any intelligence the definiteness, the
preciseness, disappear. They are in fact only on the
surface ; they only exist in the " form," the form of
words and language, which our Saviour was pleased
to adopt in speaking about the future. He employed
in part parable, in part prophecy, although the two
are not very clearly distinguished ; inasmuch as the
prophecy sometimes slides insensibly into parable.
To the parables we shall return presently. It is
necessary to point out here concerning the prophecies
that they are moulded on those of the Old Testament, and have essentially the same character—as
we might have expected. Take any Old Testament
prophecy of the last things, such, *e.g.*, as that in
Micah v. It is a very splendid piece of writing :
it is exceedingly effective, highly rhetorical, and
withal truly poetic. It conveys a very strong impres-
ison ; an impression which is in one way extremely
definite. God is to be glorified and exalted : God's
people are to be delivered and exalted too : wickedness is to perish for evermore : righteousness and
peace and joy are to have full accomplishment and
sway. All that is exceedingly definite—as definite
as it is satisfactory. If the mind is delighted with
the mingled beauty and dignity and quaintness of
the language, the soul is equally delighted with the
splendour of the hope, of the promise, conveyed.

But in another way there is nothing definite
about the prophecy at all. Examine the passage ;

examine it in connection with its context—just where it lies in the page of Scripture. Almost invariably you find that this magnificent prophecy is closely connected with some political occurrence, some temporal deliverance, which was to occur (and did occur) in the then immediate future. Let us say that it is—as indeed it very often is—the return from Babylon. Well, you cannot with any sort of satisfaction cut the passage up, and say, "This verse speaks of the return to Judæa, and that verse of the days of the Messiah, or of the times of refreshing which are to come from the presence of the Lord." Both elements are there, but so inextricably mixed that they cannot be disentangled. It belonged to the "prophetic perspective" of these great writers that they foresaw the glories of the Messiah and of His Kingdom in close relation to, in close connection with, some approaching deliverance or triumph of Israel; and they prophesied accordingly, apparently quite unaware of the immense tract of time which was to intervene. That was the method of the Holy Ghost "who spake by the Prophets." If we were petulant enough to insist that there was error and deception in it, unworthy of the Spirit of God, we should only advertise our own ignorance and presumption. It is no doubt a far more beautiful and useful method than we should ever have thought out. But it has of course this "disadvantage" (as men have been ever tempted to consider it) that it makes the interpretation of prophecy impossible, as far as time and place and outward circumstance are concerned. All the ap-

M

pearance of definiteness which many of these
prophecies possess is appearance only ; it belongs
to their form, not their substance. Only history,
only experience, could unravel the twisted threads
and make known how much in the prophecy
belonged to the *immediate* future, and how much
to the *final* future—the Kingdom of Heaven. Now
it is precisely the same with prophecies of the end
as spoken by our Lord. The Holy Ghost has not,
in fact, changed His method. In the great eschatological discourse of St. Matthew xxiv., *e.g.*, our Lord
speaks at once of the destruction of Jerusalem and
the end of the world, and connects the two events
(thus intimately conjoined) with His own coming to
judgment. The acutest commentators have given up
the attempt to disentangle the double reference
which runs right through the prophecy. It cannot
in fact be done except after a fashion which is
quite arbitrary, and therefore quite irreverent. It
may be noted in passing that while " destructive "
criticism is often sadly irreverent, there is a criticism
which calls itself "conservative" or "orthodox,"
which surpasses all other for sheer irreverence : for
it does not stick at treating our Lord's words with
the most outrageous violence in order to force them
into conformity with some traditional opinion as to
what He "must" have meant. It is reverence as
well as truth to say that our Lord was apparently
unaware of the enormous tract of time which was
to separate the fall of Jerusalem from the end of the
world. Whether He was *really* unaware, or not, we
need not here enquire. Without doubt He spake

as if He were : He gave no hint that the two events
would lie absolutely apart in time and circumstance.
The Holy Ghost spake by Him concerning the immediate and the final future exactly as He had
spoken by the prophets of old. Whatever indirect
effect (if any) this fact may have upon our ways
of thinking and of speaking about the mystery
of the Incarnation, we ought to recognize the fact.
The prophecies of our Lord create a tremendously
deep and definite impression—an impression which
is, of course, profoundly true ; but they do not lend
themselves in the very least to the purpose of those
people who want to lay them out in chart and
diagram, in time and place and detail. Those
people found themselves mistaken at the very first,
in the most crucial point of all. He did not come
when He seemed to say that He would. It is surely
a sufficiently certain inference from this undoubted
fact that whenever people try to turn our Lord's
prophecies into definite predictions (definite, *i.e.*, as
to time or place or detail) they will be equally
mistaken. The attempt is founded upon an erroneous
conception of the nature of prophecy to which we
surely ought to have had our eyes opened by this
time. The actually and definitely predictive element
in these prophecies is after all exceedingly small.
It is limited to the one fact (of inexhaustible import)
that our Lord will come again and bring with Him
the fulness of the Kingdom. All the rest is simply
the setting of this one fact—a setting which has
no other object than to throw it up in the most vivid
and emphatic relief. If anyone thinks such an

estimate derogatory, it must be because he has not studied the Old Testament—because he declines to "hear Moses and the prophets." The one and only lesson of heavenly wisdom which the Church has ever learnt from these prophecies of our Lord's is this, that His Return is for all religious purposes *the next thing*—the one thing upon which every faithful servant of His has to keep his eyes steadily fixed. For the true servant of Christ there is not any earthly to-morrow: each day runs right on without a break into the Day which shall try all its work and crown all its patience in the Presence of the Master Himself. The Saviour of the world stands as it were upon the mountain ridge whence He ascended into Heaven. We have gone in the freshness and fervour of our faith to see Him off, to bid Him good-bye for "the little while" of which He spake. It is early dawn, and the mists lie thick and white upon the levels and the lower slopes. Away to the east there is another mountain ridge of uncertain height and distance. The growing intensity of light behind it, and the marvellous transparency of the air, make it seem very distinct and vastly nearer than it is. The highest crest has caught the sunshine, and takes on a sudden splendour. The Saviour points to it. "Behold," He says, "My Second Coming: it is there already, it looks you in the face, it is at hand: remember the words that I spake unto you." And so He has blessed us, and He is gone: and we set our faces to the east, and our eyes are on the shining ridge which looks so near just now: and down below the mists lie close and quiet over the endless plains and dreary deserts and tangled forests and stony ridges which lie between. By-and-by the mists will rise, and as we go down into these interminable distances we shall take note that the Saviour said nothing about *them*, almost made as if *they* did not exist. But we know that He spake true when He ignored everything else, and pointed right away and across to His Second Coming, because He has the words of eternal life—and eternal life knows not death, and does not care for lapse of time.

It may perhaps be urged that such a statement of the case takes no account of the revelation given to St. John in Patmos. But the truth is that the strange light — a light from Heaven itself—which shines in the Apocalypse, shines upon the upper surface only of the mists which lie so still and close upon the course of history between our Lord's going and His Return. The light never gets beneath the mists, it only plays upon their upper surface with effects which are sometimes bright and beautiful, sometimes weird and terrible. These effects of heavenly light upon the earth-born mists have wonderful lessons in the heart of them. But they do not teach us any earthly history, or anything resembling it. That is not God's purpose.

XIV

THE PARABLE OF THE TEN VIRGINS

St. Matthew xxv. 1-12.

Then shall the kingdom of heaven be likened unto ten virgins, which took their lamps, and went forth to meet the bridegroom. And five of them were wise, and five were foolish. They that were foolish took their lamps, and took no oil with them : but the wise took oil in their vessels with their lamps. While the bridegroom tarried, they all slumbered and slept. And at midnight there was a cry made, Behold, the bridegroom cometh ; go ye out to meet him. Then all those virgins arose, and trimmed their lamps. And the foolish said unto the wise, Give us of your oil ; for our lamps are gone out. But the wise answered, saying, Not so ; lest there be not enough for us and you : but go ye rather to them that sell, and buy for yourselves. And while they went to buy, the bridegroom came ; and they that were ready went in with him to the marriage ; and the door was shut. Afterward came also the other virgins, saying, Lord, Lord, open to us. But he answered and said, Verily I say unto you, I know you not.

THIS parable is by universal admission wonderful and effective to the last degree. It is very picturesque, and lends itself to any amount of word painting and picture painting. It is thoroughly dramatic, full of action, and of passion too. How many thousands have been moved to tears by the late Poet Laureate's lines, subdued and restrained as they are ! " The door was shut." There is a stern, hard hopelessness about the words which is ineffably sad, and when we apply them to eternal things we absolutely shudder at what they seem to say so clearly. But then it is not clear that we have any right to apply them to eternal things, at least in any direct way. For the more frankly we consider the parable the more impossible is it to accept that view of it which underlies the ordinary "pulpit" rendering of it. According to this view, the parable is a thinly-veiled description of what will really happen to ourselves, and to other members of the Christian community, when Christ comes again. The Bridegroom is our Lord. The wise virgins are good Christians; the foolish virgins are careless Christians. The lamps represent the "holy living and godliness" by which we ought to be distinguished; the oil that grace of the Holy Spirit without which this light cannot be maintained. The going in of the wise to the wedding feast is Heaven; the shutting out of the foolish is hell. That is simple and, by virtue of the ease and effect with which it can be applied, attractive. But it is absolutely fatal to it that the character of the wise virgins, as shown by their conduct, is utterly un-Christian. From the point of view of the Gospel they are distinctly worse than the others. The only fault charged against the foolish virgins is "foolishness," want of foresight, carelessness. The wise virgins are simply wise in their own interests; they are selfish, and hard-hearted. They decline to part with any of their oil, for fear they should not have enough left for themselves; they get rid of the disagreeable importunity of their sisters by sending them to buy oil at the shops—in the middle of the night! Now there is no need to blame the

wise virgins—not the least. Our Lord has evidently
no intention whatever of blaming them. They only
behaved as the ordinary run of people would behave
under such circumstances. They belong essentially
to the natural, unregenerate, non - moral, world.
They are only thinking of themselves. It does not
occur to them, with the pleasures of the marriage
feast in view, to be generous—much less to be
deliberately self-sacrificing. Why should it ? They
are not Christians, and they do not stand for
Christians except in one specific and very limited
aspect. They are just part of a story from common
human life, as seen in the east—like the unrighteous
steward, or the unjust judge. These last indeed are
distinctly *immoral*, whereas the wise virgins are only
unmoral; but the one fact is just as fatal as the other
to any attempt to read into the story the essential
conditions and distinctions of Christianity. For
Christianity is nothing if it is not moral: and
Christian morality is nothing if it is not self-forgetful
and self-sacrificing. The supreme law of it, as laid
down by our Lord Himself in this very Gospel,[1]
requires of us a willingness to forfeit our own " souls "
for the sake of love and duty. It is indeed astonishing (and disgraceful too) how the ingenuity of man
has contrived to twist our Lord's words into something not only different but actually opposite. By
the simple device of translating the same Greek
word, in the same immediate context, by two
different English words — " life " and " soul " — and
then persistently treating these English words as

[1] Matt. xvi. 25, 26.

having a totally distinct reference, we have contrived to make Him preach the Gospel, so familiar and so dear to many of us, of "enlightened selfishness." "You must be prepared," we make Him say, "to give up everything here, even your very *life*, that you may save your *soul;* it will be a bargain well worth making, for what can compare in value to your immortal soul? and what good would it be, if you lived in all magnificence, and lost your soul, and so went to hell?"

Thousands of sermons are preached every week to that effect; and those who preach them, if they know anything of the New Testament, know that it is absolutely impossible that our Lord could have meant anything of the sort. "Life" and "soul" in this passage are identical, whichever word we may elect to use. Nor (if we prefer "life") is it life in its material aspects, but in its immaterial and eternal. It is the same word used in this Gospel when our Lord says, "Fear not them that kill the body, but are not able to kill the *soul*";[1] and again, "Ye shall find rest unto your *souls*."[2] It would indeed be more in keeping with our present use of language to translate it "soul" in the passage we are considering, for it means "life" in the highest and deepest sense. Anyhow the object of our Lord in St. Matthew xvi. 26 is certainly *not* (as the A.V. suggests without a shadow of excuse) to exalt the soul as compared with the life, but to magnify the greatness of the sacrifice demanded in the previous verse. A man who has the Spirit of Christ must

---

[1] Matt. x. 28.   [2] Matt. xi. 29.

be prepared to lose even his life, or soul; a stupendous sacrifice indeed, for what can conceivably be more precious to him than his life, or soul! But so it is. When a man is really possessed with the spirit of self-sacrifice, which is the Spirit of Christ, he does not make bargains, or draw lines. He does not say, "I will give up so much in this world, because it will be worth my while; but I will not surrender aught in the world to come, because I cannot afford to." It does not occur to him, generally speaking, to conceive that any surrender of eternal things could do any good to anyone else, or redound to the glory of Christ; but if perchance it *does* occur to him, he does not shrink from it. St. Paul is himself a case in point, and a witness unto us. "I could wish that I myself were anathema from Christ for my brethren's sake."[1] No ingenuity can get rid of or even soften down that "anathema from Christ." It meant all, and more than all, that we could possibly understand by losing our own souls. Yet he felt that he could welcome that doom, so unspeakably awful, for himself, if only it would help to save his brethren. That it would not help is nothing to the point; he meant it; and so would anyone else who was really possessed by the Spirit of Christ.

It follows then for certain that the conduct of the wise virgins was most unchristian. Instead of saying "Peradventure there will not be enough for us and you" — which is the language of purely selfish cautiousness—they should have said, "We are not

[1] Rom. ix. 3.

sure that there is enough for all of us, but see—we
will take the risk and share it with you." Nay,
they might have said, "There may not be enough
for all, but you shall have our lamps which are full,
and we will stay outside if it must be so." It is
no answer to this to say that the oil represents the
grace of God and cannot be given away by one
Christian to another. The wise virgins did not say
they *could* not part with their oil, but that they
would not. Their language was clearly and unmistakably the language of an odious selfishness,
which thought of nothing but its own profit and
security. It is quite open to a good Christian to
say that, if this parable is a representation of what
will happen at the last Day, he would rather take
his chance outside with the foolish virgins than go
in with the wise ones. If our Lord's teaching means
anything, it certainly means that it is a less evil
in His sight to be careless and foolish than to be
selfish and ungenerous. When we compare Scribes
and Pharisees with publicans and harlots, we know
perfectly well which of these two sorts of people
our Lord had most hope of. It is only possible
to conclude that, in spite of all appearances to the
contrary, this parable does not represent the great
division of the last Day except in one very definite
and very limited particular. The wise virgins do
not stand for the saved, nor the foolish for the lost,
neither does the fate of the latter throw any clear
light upon the final lot of the wicked. It is again,
like the parable of the unjust steward and so many
others, a story of earthly things and earthly people,

the vivid colouring and dramatic interest of which
is used by our Lord to illustrate the Kingdom of
Heaven in one particular aspect of it. If anyone
thinks that the parable is *too* solemn, its colouring
too vivid, its interest *too* dramatic, to allow us so
to limit its scope, let him consider again the parable
of the unmerciful servant which has avowedly no
object but to inculcate upon Christians a forgiving
temper. When our Lord had some such necessary
thing to inculcate He never seemed to think that
any language could be too dramatic, too realistic,
too awful in its suggestions. So it is here. The
endeavour to interpret the parable theologically has
been always a failure, because it refuses to lend itself
to such interpretation without forcing, even if the
great moral difficulty to which we have drawn
attention could be got over. It is not even in
praise of watchfulness in the ordinary sense. The
wise virgins "slumbered and slept" as much as the
foolish—a saying which some of the commentators
in their despair are reduced to interpreting of the
sleep of death! Apparently that touch is introduced
in order to heighten the effect of the oil—the reserve
of oil—which the wise had, the possession of which
alone differentiated them from the foolish. You can
slumber and sleep as much as you please, if you
have oil in your vessels. The uproar is sure to
wake you in plenty of time to trim your lamp and
join the procession. What *is* the reserve of oil?
It is not possible to lay in a supply of the Holy
Spirit, and then go to sleep. So all that line of
interpretation, however attractive, must be dismissed.

Perhaps there is no interpretation which can be put into the technical language of theology. But on the other hand everyone knows that there are people who *have* in themselves reserves of spiritual strength and grace upon which they *can* draw in the hour of need. In ordinary times and under negative conditions (as of night) their superiority is not manifest; but it is there, and when it is wanted it will appear. Any hour of danger and of trial brings it out into the open. The call to martyrdom gives it its greatest distinction in this world. But the Coming of the Lord will be the absolute test of it. We understand, even from what we know of people now, that His Presence would reveal at once an extraordinary difference between very many who now look so much alike. In some there are the reserves of grace and strength, deep down perhaps within their truest selves, upon which they would instantly draw, and so be found standing quite naturally, without confusion, before His Face. In others there are no such reserves—all their grace and strength just goes to maintain a sufficient appearance now and no more. That will make all the difference, undoubtedly: though what the difference will mean of loss and sorrow to the foolish the parable does not help us really to say. It presents that loss and sorrow under the most pathetic aspect possible, but not in language which can be converted into dogma.

XV.

THE PARABLE OF THE TALENTS

St. Matthew xxv. 14–30.

For the kingdom of heaven is as a man travelling into a far country, who called his own servants, and delivered unto them his goods. And unto one he gave five talents, to another two, and to another one : to every man according to his several ability ; and straightway took his journey. Then he that had received the five talents went and traded with the same, and made them other five talents. And likewise he that had received two, he also gained other two. But he that had received one went and digged in the earth, and hid his lord's money. After a long time the lord of those servants cometh, and reckoneth with them. And so he that had received five talents came and brought other five talents, saying, Lord, thou deliveredst unto me five talents : behold, I have gained beside them five talents more. His lord said unto him, Well done, thou good and faithful servant : thou hast been faithful over a few things, I will make thee ruler over many things : enter thou into the joy of thy lord. He also that had received two talents came and said, Lord, thou deliveredst unto me two talents : behold, I have gained two other talents beside them. His lord said unto him, Well done, good and faithful servant ; thou hast been faithful over a few things, I will make thee ruler over many things : enter thou into the joy of thy lord. Then he which had received the one talent came and said, Lord, I knew thee that thou art an hard man, reaping where thou hast not sown, and gathering where thou hast not strawed : and I was afraid, and went and hid thy talent in the earth : lo, there thou hast that is thine. His lord answered and said unto him, Thou wicked and slothful servant, thou knewest that I reap where I sowed not, and gather where I have not strawed : thou oughtest therefore to have put my money to the exchangers, and then at my coming I should have received mine own with usury. Take therefore the talent from him, and give it unto him which hath ten talents. For unto every one that hath shall be given, and he shall

have abundance : but from him that hath not shall be taken away even
that which he hath. And cast ye the unprofitable servant into outer
darkness : there shall be weeping and gnashing of teeth.

IT is an extraordinary testimony to the force of
our Lord's teaching, and to the hold it has taken
upon the minds of English-speaking people, that
the word "talent," which meant nothing in His day
but a sum of money, should for us have no other
meaning than that of mental endowment. There is
nothing to account for the change but this parable :
and not the parable itself as a story, but the interpretation of it as it has become the common property
of common people. The word has taken on its
present familiar signification by a process which is
purely Scriptural and evangelical. True, there is a
certain narrowness in our use of the word which is
instructive. The talents of the parable did not stand
for mental endowments more than for any other gifts,
capacities, powers, entrusted to our keeping. Yet
amongst all the gifts for which man is responsible,
mental endowments are in fact so far and away the
most valuable and effective that the limitation may
be pardoned. Much more serious, because diametrically opposed to the true lesson of the parable,
is the tendency to think of "talents" as a man's
personal possession for which he may be praised or
envied. Nevertheless the word itself is a singular
testimony to the readiness with which the English-
speaking people have accepted those great ideas of
responsibility, of fidelity to trust, of strenuousness in
the use of advantages, which form the backbone of

their moral character and the secret of their greatness. It is indeed a pity that they so often forget
that all these ideas are our Lord's, and have no other
source or sanction than in His teaching. That any
mental endowment is a "talent," and therefore to be
made the very most of, belongs to the vocabulary of
the Kingdom of Heaven, and no one can use the
word without coming under obligation to the Parables
of the Kingdom.

That we do so use this word, habitually, is a
testimony to the fact that the lesson of the Parable
of the Talents is very easy to grasp as well as one
which commends itself to the national character.
Had the point been less obvious, had it required any
elaborate explanation, or indeed any explanation at
all, it is hardly possible that the sum and substance
of it should have passed with a single word into our
common language. In this case, at any rate, it has
been instinctively perceived that the parable does not
intimate a transaction so much as inculcate a temper.
That we all have one Master: that we have nothing
but what we have received : that we are to make
faithful and strenuous use of the capacities and
opportunities entrusted to us ; all this is so graphic-
ally illustrated, and is itself so simple and obvious,
that no one has ever missed it. To the British mind,
which is slow and unimaginative and very limited in
many ways, yet capable of grasping simple ideas
very strongly, this is perhaps the ideal parable. It
is precisely suited to a "nation of shopkeepers," and
anticipates in a singular manner the modern feeling
about banks and the duty of making the most of

money. The commercial tone of the parable is indeed remarkable. In the Old Testament taking interest upon money is looked upon with horror. It is a thing which no good man will dream of doing. In the parable it is the ordinary and natural thing to do, and the failure to do it is little less than criminal neglect. It is true that this cannot be pressed in favour of "usury," because it may be argued that the lord of the parable is only one of the great men of this world, and is represented as acting just as one of them might be expected to act. But on the other hand it is clear that he is identified with the Lord Himself in an unusual degree, and his words are at times the very words of Christ. It is difficult not to refer the "well done, good and faithful servant," and the "enter thou into the joy of thy lord," to Him whose we are and whom we serve. It is almost inevitable therefore that the commercial tone of the parable should be considered as reflecting His mind, and this tone is altogether acceptable to the English-speaking people. To waste money, or not to make full and careful use of it, whether in one's own behalf, or in behalf of those to whom one is responsible— this is dreadful in our eyes. No parable, therefore, has taken hold of us quite so much as this, for it is exactly level to our thoughts.

One thing only seems to detract from the wonderful effectiveness of the parable. The wicked and slothful servant is represented, somewhat elaborately, as acting as he does under the influence of fear and dislike. At any rate that is the excuse he makes, and the excuse is not declared to be false. On the contrary

N

it is accepted as true, and shown to be a reason for
the greater carefulness. Now it is the universal conviction that the "unprofitable servant" neglects his
Master's interests almost always out of idleness,
indifference, self-indulgence—not out of dislike or
fear. No doubt there are a few who do really look
upon our Lord as "an austere man," as One who has
taken the old light-hearted joyousness and *"abandon"*
out of human life, and replaced it by a dismal ideal
of self-sacrifice and asceticism. And these few have
learnt to express their dislike of Him without mitiga-
tion or remorse. But their attitude is not at all that
of the slothful servant in the parable. They do not
propose to keep their talent laid up in order to be
returned to the Giver: they propose to make the
very utmost of it in the service of another master.
It would in fact be almost impossible to find anybody
at the present time who at all accurately corresponded
to that servant. He does not seem to be drawn from
real life. It is practically impossible to regard our
Lord as hard, exacting, and unfair towards His own
servants; and the temptation to make that an excuse
for doing nothing scarcely exists. If the servant had
said, "Lord, thou gavest me but one talent and it did
not seem worth while to do anything with it because
it meant so very little," we should have recognized
the type at once: as it is, we may say that this is
what he really meant, but we have no authority
whatever for saying so. There are a dozen very
common faults of character which would have
produced the same bad conduct—idleness, slack-
ness, bad temper, envy, and so forth; but our Lord

has left them all out, and indicated another which is almost unknown. That slavish attitude of mind, of which the dominant principle is fear and personal dislike, so accentuated as to make a man reckless even of his own interests, is quite foreign to Christianity. The disposition to presume upon our Lord's goodness has always been incalculably stronger than the disposition to exaggerate His severity. It is no use trying to conceal this fact from ourselves, and therefore we are driven to suppose that the bad servant was not intended to represent any class of people in the Church. He stands in the parable simply as a foil to the faithful servants. His having only one talent entrusted to him is not meant to suggest an excuse (for there is no hint that it was so regarded or alleged), but to aggravate his fault. He was only asked to take a little pains, and make the best of a small amount of property; and he would not even do that. His surliness and churlishness form the dark shadow which is necessary to throw up into relief the eager and patient fidelity of his fellow-servants. Like other dark shadows its destiny is to pass into the outer gloom, whither all sorrow and sighing shall flee away, where weeping and gnashing of teeth shall find their home. The casting out of the unprofitable servant is a dramatic incident of the story which cannot be directly interpreted any more than the taking away of his talent and the giving of it to another. No one has ever suggested any process whereby the gifts and graces originally entrusted to one man can be transferred to another. The wasted life of a man cannot be made

use of by anybody else. Again it is abundantly
evident that in this part of the parable we have not
(as many have supposed) a thinly veiled representation
of our Christian probation: we have only a story
whose picturesque incidents suggest certain lessons
of the Christian life—lessons which do not altogether
lie upon the surface or in the letter. If however we
leave the slothful servant on one side, we are justified
in saying that no parable lends itself more naturally
or more safely to direct and simple application than
this. The plain duties of life, the true rewards of
Heaven, are here more distinctly set before us than
(perhaps) anywhere else. Nowhere is the great trial
of Christian living and working so clearly indicated
—the fact, namely, that we are so very much left to
ourselves, and that for so long a time. Nowhere is
the supreme reward more clearly shown to lie in the
Master's satisfaction with our work and the Master's
commendation of ourselves. Once and for all the
parable puts us unmistakably in our true relationship to Him for time and for eternity. From this
point of view there is not another parable of the
Kingdom to equal it.

XVI.

THE PARABLE OF THE SHEEP AND GOATS

St. Matthew xxv. 31-46.

When the Son of man shall come in his glory, and all the holy angels with him, then shall he sit upon the throne of his glory : And before him shall be gathered all nations : and he shall separate them one from another, as a shepherd divideth his sheep from the goats : And he shall set the sheep on his right hand, but the goats on the left. Then shall the King say unto them on his right hand, Come, ye blessed of my Father, inherit the kingdom prepared for you from the foundation of the world : For I was an hungred, and ye gave me meat : I was thirsty, and ye gave me drink : I was a stranger, and ye took me in : naked, and ye clothed me : I was sick, and ye visited me : I was in prison, and ye came unto me. Then shall the righteous answer him, saying, Lord, when saw we thee an hungred, and fed thee? or thirsty, and gave thee drink? When saw we thee a stranger, and took thee in? or naked, and clothed thee? Or when saw we thee sick, or in prison, and came unto thee? And the King shall answer and say unto them, Verily I say unto you, Inasmuch as ye have done it unto one of the least of these my brethren, ye have done it unto me. Then shall he say also unto them on the left hand, Depart from me, ye cursed, into everlasting fire, prepared for the devil and his angels : For I was an hungred, and ye gave me no meat : I was thirsty, and ye gave me no drink : I was a stranger, and ye took me not in : naked, and ye clothed me not : sick, and in prison, and ye visited me not. Then shall they also answer him, saying, Lord, when saw we thee an hungred, or athirst, or a stranger, or naked, or sick, or in prison, and did not minister unto thee? Then shall he answer them, saying, Verily I say unto you, Inasmuch as ye did it not to one of the least of these, ye did it not to me. And these shall go away into everlasting punishment : but the righteous into life eternal.

IT is of course uncertain whether we ought to call it a parable at all. From a purely literary point of view the element of parable is reduced to the barest minimum. It is only in a single sentence that the sheep and the goats take the place of the human beings whose destiny our Lord is declaring: "And he shall set the sheep on his right hand, but the goats on his left."[1] Before this they have only been introduced by way of illustration : after this they are mentioned no more. It is not possible to imagine a "parable" in which the pictorial form should be more slight and transient than in this. Only for one brief moment do we see the sheep and the goats, which all day long have been intermixed, drafted out and separated by the shepherd ; and even in seeing them for that moment we know already that they represent the final severance of saints and sinners. Yet this momentary representation is in itself so striking, and has so powerfully laid hold of the imagination of mankind, that it gives a certain colour to the whole of this discourse. So much is implied in it, so much is suggested by it, that all the time we listen to the story of judgment and of doom we are thinking more or less definitely of the sheep and the goats. Other and deeper reasons there are for considering it a parable—but this would itself be enough. Before we go any further, therefore, it will be worth while to consider more attentively what is really involved in this remarkable comparison. Instinctively we assume that the sheep is good, and the goat bad. There seems good reason for this assumption in that the goats are placed on the shepherd's left hand where the wicked are afterwards found. But there is no other reason. In the

[1] Matt. xxv. 33.

Old Testament sheep and goats are placed upon a perfect equality for religious, *i.e.* for sacrificial, purposes. The very Paschal "lamb," which more than any other dumb animal represented Christ, might be taken "from the sheep or from the goats":[1] in other words, it was just as likely to be a kid as a lamb. The same word stood for either. He-goats and rams were both used as symbols of violent and aggressive people or powers : but there is no trace of any moral distinction between the two animals in the Old Testament. No doubt it is often the case that sheep are white and goats are black, and when they are mixed the contrast of colour is extremely marked. But sometimes the contrast is just the other way. In parts of South Africa the goats have beautifully white fleeces, while the sheep around them are almost quite black from the burnt grass over which they feed. Nor is there any reason to think that the Jews associated moral qualities with white and black as we have learnt to do. There was no shadow of reproach connected with the name or thought of a goat. It seems to follow therefore that nothing of the kind is implied in the comparison used by our Lord. Whichever one may prefer, sheep and goats *are* markedly different in appearance, and because they differ so much in appearance it is easy and natural to separate them. There is no fear of making any mistake, or overlooking any stray individual. The whole point lies in the sharpness of distinction which leads to an equal sharpness of division. That the goats are placed by the shepherd

[1] Exodus xii. 5.

on his left hand has in it nothing derogatory to them : as far as they are concerned it is accidental, and has no significance.

Now we leave this illustration, so brief and slight but so picturesque, and turn to the narrative itself which it serves to illustrate. For, a narrative it has all the appearance of being : a narrative of things to come indeed, but a narrative plain and straight-forward and simple, which comes to us from the lips and on the authority of Him who is Shepherd, Judge, and King, who is without doubt to be the arbiter and disposer of our eternal destinies. When He casts aside the similitudes and parables which He has used so long to teach us the truth about His Kingdom ; when He tells us plainly, in language of awful solemnity, how He is going to deal with men in the last Day; what have we to do but to believe Him and to accept His words in their most literal and obvious sense ? And this has been done —quite rightly done. Who can possibly know what the Son of man will do when He comes in His glory except the Son of man Himself? And if He choose to tell us that He will act thus and thus, who are we that we should say it is incredible, impossible ? Accordingly almost all men have agreed to find in this sublime discourse a plain account of what will happen when Christ comes again to judge the world. Nevertheless, the difficulties are so enormous, so over-whelming, that it is at least necessary to suspend our judgment until we have fairly weighed them. If it should after all appear that, in the face of the New Testament teaching generally, this description of the final division of mankind cannot be literally accepted, then we shall be compelled—not indeed for one moment to disbelieve our Lord, but—to understand that He is still speaking to us in the parables and figures which He had seemed (but only seemed) to have laid aside.

The first great difficulty which emerges from this description of Judgment to come is that it is Judgment by works, and by works exclusively. True, this difficulty is constantly meeting us all through the New Testament. It is so clearly the teaching of Scripture that we have put it into our creeds as a foundation truth. "They that have done good shall go into life everlasting; and they that have done evil into everlasting fire." "This," we say, "is the Catholic Faith" which it is absolutely needful to hold. Nor can anyone deny that it is true, without directly contradicting the Scripture. But it is quite open to us to affirm that while Judgment by works is a plain doctrine of Scripture, Salvation by faith is equally plain — and by no ingenuity can the two be reconciled now. Doubtless in the ultimate working out of things which belongs to God and to eternity they *will* be reconciled. But in creeds and confessions they remain, and must remain, incongruous and incompatible. We can, all of us, perfectly understand and absolutely accept Judgment by works. The thought of it is quite familiar by reason of our earthly experience. The expectation of it is quite natural by reason of our instinctive demand for justice. The strength of that demand is artificially weakened in our own case by the exceptional ease and safety of our lot. We can scarcely realize the fact that the great majority lack justice even more than they lack food, and suffer more from unrighteous treatment than they do from hunger and want. But we have only to turn to the Psalms to see that the demand for *justice* is the most general and imperious of all the religious demands of men at large. Men have needed God, not in the first instance to show mercy upon themselves, but to avenge them of unrighteousness and wrong, and to vindicate outraged innocence. The Psalms of vengeance, which we find so alien to our own religious temper, are the expression (quite legitimate in its way, and quite inevitable) of this primary passion of the soul—for justice. The Lord God Himself must justify His existence by clearing the innocent and confounding the guilty. How else shall any man know, to any good purpose, that there *is* a God that judgeth the earth? Nor is it otherwise with that cry of martyred lives (" lives," not souls, for the life of a living creature is in the blood thereof, and it is the blood which is poured away "underneath the altar ") which has seemed so out of place occurring where it does, "how long, O Master, holy and true, dost Thou not judge and avenge our blood on them that dwell on the earth?"[1] To ask justice of God is even more necessary than to ask mercy. And if justice for others, why, justice for oneself too ! No one who has any loftiness of mind wants to find any respect of persons in his own favour, or asks to go to Heaven if *he ought not to be there.* "Judge me,

[1] Rev. vi. 10.

O God," is the natural cry of the soul which has any uprightness left in it. Whatever the result may be, and howsoever sorrowful; at any cost, judge me, O God, according to Thine unerring knowledge and Thy perfect righteousness. It is before all things necessary to escape once and for ever from the false judgments due to one's own self-conceit and to the too good opinion of one's friends. In the most developed stage of religious sentiment, as in the least developed, the primary demand of the soul of man upon God is for justice. So it is that all men understand and acquiesce in Judgment by works, and would not be content without it, because it means justice. But the moment that instinctive demand is satisfied, another arises, as urgent, as imperious, and takes the place of the former. Salvation by faith is just as necessary as Judgment by works, and just as much a part of our religion. Those that seek mercy shall find it, those that lay hold upon the gracious promises of God in Christ shall have those promises more than made good to them. No one can be lost that throws himself unreservedly, even at the eleventh hour, upon the Saviour's mercy. "Whosoever shall call upon the name of the Lord shall be saved."[1] But it is certainly the fact (however unwilling we may be to admit it) that we never can combine in thought these two truths; never can frame an expectation of the future which shall unite them. Both are stated, quite broadly and unreservedly, in the New Testament: are stated unequivocally, and are left to

[1] Acts ii. 21 ; Rom. x. 13.

themselves. Sometimes the Church or the individual
is led to dwell more upon the one, sometimes more
upon the other. But both are there, and both are
true; and they cannot possibly be reconciled by
human thought, however much we may try. The
way to test general principles is to apply them to
individuals. Take the following case. There was
in a certain city a heathen judge who for his own
base ends persecuted a poor widow who was a
Christian, and brought her to ruin and to death.
Now it happened that the judge was struck with
mortal sickness, and felt a certain remorse for his
evil deeds. So he sent for a Christian priest, believed
and was baptized, and washed away his sins, calling
upon the name of the Lord. Following these two
to Judgment we are *obliged* to believe (with a conviction which nothing can shake) that *both* of them
will be placed on the right hand, and will receive
that blessing which God's well-beloved Son will then
pronounce to all that love and fear Him. To say
otherwise—even to hint the least doubt—would be
tantamount to declaring ourselves not Christians at
all, but followers of some other cult altogether. No
doubt some will say that the judge will have a very
long time in purgatory, by reason of his many sins,
whereas the woman will go straight to glory by
reason of her sufferings. But, confessedly, all that
is pious opinion and lies absolutely outside the
teaching of our Lord or of His apostles. Our Lord
in His doctrine knows nothing about purgatory, and
nothing about the intermediate state. He looks
straight across to His Second Coming and the Day

when He shall sit upon the Throne of His glory, and in that day He will judge all men according to their works.   Nevertheless the wicked judge will go into life everlasting along with the widow whom he persecuted unto death.   We are not saved by works, but by faith—which faith may *or may not* have time and opportunity to show its true nature by the works which spring from it.   We readily and joyfully understand how the penitent robber was saved by faith : how he will be judged by works no man can ever understand as long as the world endures.

There is indeed a third doctrine taught in the New Testament which *partially* reconciles these other two, and doubtless points to the ultimate and perfect reconciliation of them.   That is salvation by mystical union with Christ — a union which involves the affections and the will and all the deepest springs of character and motive out of which "works" must ultimately come.   This doctrine is taught by St. John and St. Paul especially, and cannot be got rid of by any natural impatience at what is occult and mystical.   Those who are "in" Christ are saved in the simple and true sense of being safe.   They have "put off" themselves and "put on" Christ.   They have entered upon joint possession and enjoyment of that which is *His*—His life, His victory, His sinlessness even.   There is a holy partnership, a *solidarité*, between Him and them.   He takes their sins, He counts their sufferings His own, He shares with them His very Throne.   They "sit in heavenly places" already "*in* Christ Jesus."[1]   All this is of

---

[1] Eph, ii. 6,

course nothing arbitrary, it is not favouritism : it implies a real unity of moral character as well as of spiritual life—however little time and opportunity the moral character may have had to assert itself. But it is evident that this doctrine, like that of salvation by faith, is incompatible with any *unqualified* belief in a universal Judgment by works. Those who *have* everlasting life because they are "in Christ" cannot be divested of that life while they stand before the Judgment Seat, and then be reinvested with it. In other words, the Judgment cannot have any real *judicial* value in their case. Their eternal future must be settled, not by anything they have done or not done, but by what they *are*. When we think about it, we all agree to this : we cannot help ourselves. Even in the case of an earthly tribunal we recognize that oftentimes it only tries and sentences people for what they have *done*, because it has no other means of knowing what they *are*. If it could discover with assurance what people *are*, we should prefer that it should make *this* the ground of its decisions. When we can we judge others by the same rule : "wherein ye were also careful, but ye lacked opportunity,"[1] says St. Paul. And so much more our Lord. If all nations are to stand before Him at the Doom, to be judged by works, to how vast a multitude must He say, "Ye never did me any good, or showed me any kindness — but ye lacked opportunity." "I was an hungred," He must say to these, "and ye gave me no meat : I was thirsty, and ye gave me no drink,

[1] Phil. iv, 10,

—but indeed I perceive that ye would have done it had it come in your way: but ye lacked opportunity." All infants of course and young children must come within this wide exception, and all others whose lives are without initiative. Nor can anyone even imagine at what stage or under what circumstances men do really pass under the law of Judgment by works. A very large proportion, perhaps the majority, must in any case stand outside it. What follows then? Surely this, that Judgment by works, although true and certain, is only one side of a tremendous verity which in its fulness is to us unimaginable. It is necessary to say (for it is the fact) that in telling us of the future our Lord is limited by the limitations of our imagination. It is no use His telling us things which we have no power to grasp; no use His leading us through tracts where the wings of human thought do not enable us to follow. *He* says it, therefore it is true, is a right conclusion. *He* says it, therefore it is the whole truth, is entirely false. He may only be able to put before us some part, some aspect, of the truth; and He may think it best to put *that* aspect before us as impressively, as dramatically, as possible. That *is*, apparently, His way. We on our part may be able to seize that aspect, although we may not be able to combine it with other aspects which are equally true. Assuredly all the references to the Judgment in the New Testament are more or less dramatic. No one now takes the details literally. No one supposes, *e.g.*, that actual "books"[1]

[1] Rev. xx. 12,

are kept in Heaven, books which will be "opened" in order that the entries may be read out. It would be as reasonable to suppose that an actual "bottle"[1] is kept in Heaven, in which the "tears" of the saints are put. Who does not see that these things, these images, belong to the *language* of inspired Scripture —language which is so wonderfully poetic, and often so essentially dramatic? What it ever aims at is *effect*: what it does is to call up an image before the mind, simple, vivid, true to the eternal fact so far as that fact can be grasped by a human mind. By means of sensible images called up in the mind it sets forth the certainty that nothing whatever will escape the knowledge, the scrutiny, the approval or disapproval, of the great Judge. All things whatever, in action or in motive, will be "naked and open before the eyes of Him with whom we" shall "have to do";[2] no injustice will escape detection, no hypocrisy remain unmasked, no self-delusion unexposed, no unfairness uncorrected. Justice, God's justice, will be manifested and vindicated absolutely. All the rest seems to belong to the dramatic setting forth of this supreme truth. There will be no possibility of concealment, of self-delusion, of false moral perspectives, of one-sided estimates. Every child of man will take his own place according to what he is. In manifesting what he is, his actions will be weighed, *so far as they are available for that purpose*, so far as they really represent his inner self. It seems impossible to doubt that this is what Judgment by works actually

[1] Psalm lvi. 8.   [2] Heb. iv. 13.

comes to as a part of our Christian expectation. It is true, for ever true—but only a part of the truth. It is not applicable to a large part of mankind, because they have no works good or bad. It is only very partially applicable to the rest, because their works do not fairly represent them : their lack of opportunity, and also their self-reproach and efforts to do better, have to be taken into account. It is not absolutely or certainly applicable to any single soul (at least on the bad side), because at the very last he may by faith leave his old self behind and find a better and truer self in Christ. Judgment by works, however much insisted on in Scripture, may never be taught as if it were a simple truth perfect in itself. It cannot in fact stand alone. It instantly topples over if we try to make it do so. It corresponds to and satisfies one imperious instinct of our human nature which belongs to its divine original. But by itself it would fail to satisfy, it would rather awake to intolerable pain, other instincts as imperious and as universal. We want justice : but we want mercy too. Above all, we want a union with God in which both justice and mercy will live, yet no longer as distinct, far less as mutually opposed, but as one and the same goodness of God.

If this be so, it follows that our Lord's discourse in the latter half of St. Matthew xxv. is not a prophetic description of what will happen at the last Day, but a dramatic presentation of Judgment intended to set forth one particular aspect of it. For it is Judgment by works and nothing else. Even

o

motives are excluded, so far as they can be accounted
Christian. For the righteous are quite ignorant that
they are succouring Christ, and the wicked that they
are neglecting Him. The division of all men into
two lots—the one for Heaven, and the other for Hell
—follows strictly and unhesitatingly the simple line
of what they have actually done or not done, just
as if there were not the slightest difficulty about it.
But we have seen that the difficulties are insuperable.
Quite reverently, on the strength of His own teaching
and the teaching of His apostles—quite reverently,
but quite certainly, we say that the truth of this
picture of Judgment is very partial and very limited.
And in practice all good Christians believe and teach
as if it were so.

For it is not only Judgment by works and nothing
else ; it is Judgment by one particular class of works
which are the outcome of a single virtue. As in the
parable of the Virgins our Lord was pleased to make
everything depend upon the possession of certain
reserves of strength and grace—which are themselves
dependent upon seriousness and foresight ; as in the
parable of the Servants He made everything turn
upon faithfulness in the use of " talents "; so now, in
the most profoundly solemn of all discourses, He
magnifies charity as the first and greatest of virtues,
in comparison with which all other virtues may (for
the moment) be ignored. But only for the moment,
and only for the sake of dramatic effect. By no
possibility can any Christian man persuade himself
that charity is the only virtue which differentiates
a saint from a sinner, or that charity is the only

virtue which Christ loves and praises. Is justice
nothing? Shall purity go for nought? Even St.
James, who preaches to us with such delightful
simplicity the old Galilean Gospel of those never-to-
be-forgotten " days of the Son of man," tells us that
pure religion and undefiled includes the keeping of
oneself unspotted from the world as well as visiting
widows and orphans.[1]   Suppose these two things the
sole constituents of acceptable religion, yet only one
of these is charity, and the two by no means always
or naturally go together.   Common experience, which
cannot be mistaken, tells us that a very loose manner
of living not at all unfrequently goes hand in hand
with a kindness of heart which is very beautiful and
admirable.   Drunkards, and harlots, and people who
do not know what truth means, will share their last
morsel with some starving wretch, and put themselves to any amount of fatigue and trouble to show
kindness to dying folk.   By all means let us praise
and magnify their charity.   It is quite impossible
to say how precious it may be in the eyes of Christ.
It may stand these poor creatures in better stead
in the Day of Judgment than all the churchgoing
and all the religious observances of the most
respectable people who had a deaf ear and a cold
heart for the sorrows of others.   We have every
reason, as Christians, to believe that such will be
the case.   We rejoice to think so.   But that is quite
another thing from affirming that charity is the only
virtue that matters : and that is what we must affirm
if we are to take our Lord literally here.   In that

[1] James i. 27.

case the moral teaching of so many modern novels is really justified. It matters not how vile and degraded a life a man may be living—how great a curse he may be to himself and his neighbours. He has left in him the power of heroic self-sacrifice for the sake of another, and in some supreme moment he puts forth that power and does some good at a great cost, probably at the cost of his life. And that is the highest level to which human life and death can reach in modern fiction. Is it possible to say that such an ideal is Christian? or that our Lord would have acknowledged it? Surely to preach habitual kindness, with occasional flashes of heroic self-devotion, is to come down from the level of Christianity, and to take up frankly with the ideals of heathenism. No doubt when we speak of virtues we must gladly agree that "the greatest of these is charity";[1] but we cannot possibly concede that charity is the only virtue, or the only virtue that will be of any value in the last Day. The fact is, as a long and wide experience has taught us, the Christian virtues are distributed in a very unexpected, and indeed inexplicable, way. There are whole nations which love and practise chastity, but have no sense of truth and do not mind how much they lie. There are other nations which are grievously unclean in private life, but have a high sense of justice and honour, and a chivalrous eagerness to champion the wrongs of others. So it is with individuals. They take the perfect code of Christ, the law of liberty, and divide it amongst them, so that

---

[1] I Cor. xiii. 13.

hardly any is complete, and hardly any wanting in some redeeming trait. So they live, and so they die. How is the great Judge to discern amongst them at the last Day? We cannot tell : we cannot even guess. But one thing we are sure of. He will not take the short and easy way of saying " never mind about anything else : if you were kind to other people, you go to the right—if not, to the left." That is impossible, because it would be unrighteous. So far as we are to be judged by our works at all, it must be by all our works ; by those which belong to justice and injustice, to purity and impurity, to courage and cowardice, to patience and despair, as well as those which can be set down to kindness and unkindness.

Some commentators, perceiving the impossibility of making charity the sole and sufficient line of demarcation among Christians, have sought to evade the difficulty by denying that the parable refers to Christians at all. Christian people, they say, will be judged by Christian standards as made known in the New Testament. But the heathen cannot be so judged because they have not known the requirements of "the law of liberty."[1] They can only be punished or rewarded according to a rule which they all understand, because it is written in their hearts. Whatever else they are ignorant of, they know they ought to be good and kind to one another, and very often they are. The barbarous people of Malta may very probably have led evil lives in many ways, but they showed "no little

---

[1] James ii. 12.

kindness" to St. Paul and his shipwrecked companions.[1] Barbarous people very generally *do* show
kindness to helpless strangers—more kindness than
can be reckoned on among Christian and civilized
folk. It is only (as a rule) when their superstitions
or their prejudices are aroused that they act otherwise. Even among Mohammedans, with all these
centuries of fanaticism behind them, the common
people are not unkind or ungenerous when left to
themselves. If individuals sin against the law of
charity, it is not that they are ignorant of it, but
that their better instincts are overborne by greed
or malice, or by a habit of cruelty deliberately
indulged. When therefore the Lord speaks of "all
the nations" being gathered before Him at the last
Day, we are to understand "all the heathen," for
this word "nations" corresponds to the ordinary
Hebrew word for "heathen,"[2] and is so translated
in Galatians i. 16, ii. 9, iii. 8, as well as in other
places of the New Testament. The ignorance of
both righteous and wicked that what they had done
(or not done) had any reference to Christ, shows
conclusively that they had not been Christians; for
any such ignorance is impossible in us, and if
expressed could only be a deplorable affectation.

Now this is plausible, but it is not convincing—
and that for many reasons. In the first place, our
Lord gives no hint that He is going to speak of the
heathen as such. The two preceding parables are
undeniably parables of the Kingdom, and this follows
them without break or pause. It would require very

---

[1] Acts xxviii. 2.   [2] גּוֹיִם

clear internal evidence to warrant us in assuming so complete a change of subject. In the second place, our Lord distinctly intimates in this same Gospel[1] that "all the nations" (the very same phrase) are to be brought into His fold by conversion, baptism and instruction — the instruction clearly including the whole moral law as laid down by Him. In speaking of the end of all things He must have anticipated that this command of His would have been obeyed and "all the nations" brought into His Kingdom. It is only possible to look upon the nations of St. Matthew xxv. 32 as still heathen by getting rid of St. Matthew xxviii. 19 —or, at least, by relegating the two passages to distinct and unconformable "strata" in our Lord's teaching. In the third place, we only thus rid ourselves of a difficulty at a tremendous sacrifice. No doubt the law of kindness is applicable to heathens— but it is even more applicable to Christians. We want it ourselves: we need to know that the test will be applied to us too: least of all men can we afford to relax our hold upon the great truth "inasmuch as ye did it unto one of these My brethren, even these least, ye did it unto Me." Notoriously that truth has been and is the inspiration of all that is most beautiful in Christian life and work, in the most backward of Christian countries as much as in the most advanced. It is so simple and so splendid. No one who believes is so without imagination as not to be able to grasp it. No imagination, however gifted, can ever exhaust its

[1] Matt. xxviii. 19, 20.

fulness or rise to the height of its significance. It transmutes into thrice-refined gold the base metal, the cheap currency, of our daily work and care and thought for others. Like the strong and bracing air of the mountains or the sea, it is a constant source of reinvigoration for those who are faint and weary in well-doing. More than anything else it supplies an exhilaration to the spiritual atmosphere in which we live and work which is for practical purposes of unspeakable importance. We do not doubt that the heathen also will have the benefit of this ever-blessed truth. The acts of kindness and of generosity which they have done, in all ignorance of Christ, will yet be accepted as done to Him, and they will know it with a joyful surprise when the time comes. But it is even more *for* us, because even more *to* us, who do know it now, and therefore already enjoy the reward in great measure. Glad indeed are we to share with all mankind—Pagan, Mohammedan, infidel—this parable ; but we cannot possibly let go our own possession of it.

To what conclusion therefore are we driven ? What but this, that our Lord's motive and purpose was not to let us into any secrets of the Last Judgment, but to glorify charity, that great and crowning virtue so dear to Him ? In our Lord's personal teaching it is the exact equivalent of 1 Corinthians xiii. in St. Paul's teaching ; or, as we might better say, of His teaching by St. Paul. No doubt it is difficult to take that view of it all at once. We cling desperately to the conviction (which is so natural and, with our training, so inevitable) that a story of Judgment to come must tell us something about Judgment to come. Only very slowly, fighting the ground inch by inch, we are driven back and back upon the only tenable position. Our Lord, desiring to pass His own eulogium upon charity as the most beautiful and the most necessary of all things which are to flourish and abound in His Kingdom, permits Himself to throw this eulogium into the form of a dramatic description of the Judgment day. It is astonishing; it would be incredible, if it were not the fact. But once we recover from our astonishment, we are easily able to receive it not only with profound reverence, but with profound gratitude also. We perceive at once that we have lost nothing. It never *did* teach us anything about the Judgment, for we never believed that active benevolence was the one virtue which would be taken into account. We always knew that the final severance for weal or woe could not run on such easy and simple lines as that would imply. We always in fact dimly recognized (though we did not like to acknowledge it) that the representation set before us was essentially dramatic, and had the limitation as well as the power which is proper to drama. We have lost nothing, and we are rid of some most tormenting difficulties.

If we accept this conclusion, at any rate provisionally, it will be very instructive to compare this passage with 1 Corinthians xiii. Each is a eulogium upon charity, and each is magnificent in its way. But the two ways are so different

St. Paul's eulogium is rhetoric, which rises into true
eloquence because such a profound conviction burns
and shines through it.   It is evident enough, even
from a literary point of view, that he is carried
beyond himself and out of himself by the fervour
of his mind.   His very style is transfigured, and
his words flow on with a swift and easy current.
We can almost see the glow which comes over his
face as his pen runs on with unwonted speed.
St. Paul's eulogium is rhetoric of a very high order,
with just that touch of exaggeration which is
necessary if one is to use the language of men.
Our Lord's eulogium is drama : it has no fervour
in it, no glow of conviction or of admiration such
as belongs to rhetoric : it is intensely solemn, with
a solemnity which darkens into an awful severity
or brightens into an exquisite tenderness.   There
is not anything like it in the world for effectiveness,
for unhesitating boldness, for simplicity of appeal
to the strongest feelings in common human nature,
for art which consists in the avoidance of art.   We
are transported to the last Assize.   The supreme
Judge is on His throne.   The whole human race
is there.   What is really on its trial, what is really
in question, is love and want of love.   But they do
not appear as virtue and vice, as good or bad traits
of character, as abstract notions.   That would have
been quite foreign to our Lord's methods of speech,
to the mental atmosphere in which He lived, to the
needs of those who heard Him.   Even for *us* it
would have been (by comparison) poor and in-
effective.   For *them* it had been practically useless.

It is the concrete, the dramatic, which only can convey the impression He desires to convey. Love and the want of love therefore appear before the Eternal Arbiter as men and women who in common life show kindness or unkindness. As in that first parable of the Sower the good seed is in an unexplained way identified with the people in whom it takes root, so here in the last and most perfect of parables the blessedness of charity is exhibited in the endless felicity of those who represent charity : and this effect is immensely heightened by the endless perdition of those who represent the lack of charity. Look at the two methods from a literary point of view, and we may say that the one is western, the other eastern : the one belongs to the people of Socrates, the other to the people of Isaiah : the one is modern, the other is primitive. From a literary point of view indeed the two methods are wide as the poles asunder, and belong to different worlds of thought (although so near in time and place). But from a religious point of view they are identical. They strike the same note, they teach the same truth, they are intended to have (and they do have) precisely the same effect. Neither lets us into any of the secrets of the final Judgment (which are in fact absolutely inscrutable); but both glorify charity as the very prince of all virtues here and now, and both go to create a spiritual atmosphere in which charity can live and move and have her being under all discouragements of this world. Our Lord's purpose and intent, equally with St. Paul's, is exhausted when He has persuaded us that charity more than anything else puts us in touch with Christ and makes us dear to Him. St. Paul seeks to do this, and does it, by a rhetorical comparison of charity with other gifts and other virtues—to the advantage of charity. Our Lord seeks to do this, and does it better still (if we may reverently say so), by a dramatic description of Judgment, in which all other virtues are left out of sight, and only charity is crowned. But drama has in it this disadvantage (if indeed it is not, from our Lord's point of view, the greatest advantage) that it cannot be translated into dogma. There is absolutely *no* dogma which emerges from this parable but that which comes out of the saying, " Inasmnch as ye did it unto one of these ye did it unto Me ": and *that* is a truth of this present life, exclusively. We are transported in a vision to the Throne of Judgment, and straightway we are sent back to our own homes, and the other homes around us. We are no wiser than we were before about the Judgment and the Eternal Future : we are infinitely wiser about the things of to-day, how we " ought to walk and to please God."[1]

Again, it is very instructive to connect and compare this parable with the other two in the same chapter[2] which precede it : for the three evidently form a trilogy the interest and importance of which rises as we go on. All three are dramatic : all three are concerned (in their dramatic form) with the end of the world, the Coming of the Son of man, the final division of mankind. If we ask ourselves what we

---

[1] I Thess. iv. I.   [2] Matt. xxv.

chiefly learn from these wonderful parables, the answer is not difficult. First, we learn to believe that beneath the apparent tameness and sameness of Christian character and conduct there is a difference which will prove in the end a crucial difference : there is a seriousness and a foresight about some to which they owe (humanly speaking) a staying power, a reserve of strength and grace, which will enable them to overcome while others fail. Secondly, we learn to believe that since as Christians we " serve the Lord Christ,"[1] it is above all things necessary that a man be found faithful to the trust reposed in him, and do his best for his Master's interests. Thirdly, we learn to believe that love is the fulfilling of the law in the widest sense, that charity never faileth to secure the most gracious approbation of our Lord, that no other virtue can compare with it in His eyes. Now all these are essentially lessons of the Kingdom, lessons for practical life, and not at all the less so because they are taught us by parables of things to come. Moreover, there is a clear progression from first to last. We begin by taking things seriously ; we go on by making a faithful use of our gifts ; we end by spending and being spent for love of others. The first delivers us from this present evil world, with its incurable triviality and shallowness. The second leaves us good and faithful servants, trained in the school of Christ, and found worthy of His high employ. The third makes us friends of God and companions of the Lord, since God is love. It is exactly the same upward progress

---

[1] Col. iii. 24.

that we find elsewhere in the New Testament: only it is presented to us in a dramatic form which even for us is much more impressive and striking than anything else could be. When we have learnt to look for nothing in the dramatic *form* but the tremendous effect which it must always have on the imagination, then we shall be able to give our minds as we ought to those unspeakably important lessons of the Kingdom which our Lord designed to teach.

If this view of these parables be accepted, it will follow that the fate of the foolish virgins, of the slothful servant, of those on the left hand, cannot be directly or literally insisted on as setting forth the destiny of lost souls. Nothing is indeed more common even now than to point to the terrible words, "depart ye cursed into the eternal fire," as if they settled for ever the endless doom of the lost. Even those who disbelieve the dogma of everlasting punishment have been wont to quibble about the word for "punishment" or the word for "everlasting." Great doctrines cannot rest upon nice distinctions of words, and minute enquiries into their precise shade of significance. It is wonderful that men have not noticed that our Lord was not speaking about "the lost" as a class, but about certain persons who had not shown personal kindness and attention to *Him* as represented by His brothers and sisters in affliction. It is a very disquieting reflection that many—so many —of those who have bandied arguments to and fro on this topic have never shown the least alacrity to succour Christ in the persons of His poor and suffer-

ing brethren. It has not occurred to them. They
had thought that our Lord was talking dogmatically
about "the lost"—with whom they had no personal
concern. Does it not stand there, they would say,
"then shall *the righteous* answer Him"? and must
not these others be *the wicked?* Yes, they are—but
they are only wicked because they neglected charity.
That and only that is charged against them. There
are no unbelievers here, no people who neglect public
worship, no drunkards, no thieves, no liars, no unclean persons—nobody at all but uncharitable people.
For the purpose of this parable they are identified
with the wicked, they are placed on the left hand, and
sent into eternal fire, because our Lord does not wish
to contemplate any virtue but charity, or any vice but
the want of it. No one has any right to alter the
most essential feature of the whole parable and to
treat any part of it as if it referred to saints and
sinners generally. Our Lord has not a word to say
here about anything but charity. If indeed anyone
can persuade himself that this will be the only test,
the only ground of division, in the last Day, then he
may without unfairness and wrong see in these words
the doom of sinners generally—but not otherwise.
If on the other hand, having considered all the
parables of the Kingdom of which this forms the
climax; having especially considered the two immediately preceding which form along with this an
evident trilogy; if, considering "all the parables,"[1]
he comes to the conclusion that their method is
essentially figurative and dramatic; then he will set

[1] Mark iv. 13, R.V.

aside any appeal to the words of cursing as if they settled the destiny of the lost. What they really settle is the eternal hatefulness of want of charity. What they damn is unkindness; and that in the highest degree, and for ever. And damnable it will be for ever and for all. Though it should be found (as, alas, it is) in ever so small a degree, and in ever so really religious a soul, it will still be damnable. And on the other hand a true self-forgetting benevolence will be lovable, and will be a thing which more than anything else accompanies salvation, should it be found in ever so fallen and otherwise lost a creature. It will not be irreverent to compare with our Lord's parable that story which is told in the life of the old Celtic saint Brendan. However far below, however lacking in authority or inspiration, it is yet (from the literary point of view) of the same order. It is the praise of charity thrown into an extremely bold dramatic form which takes us into the realm and region of eternal punishment. St. Brendan was sailing in the northern seas in search of some island or shore where he might preach the unsearchable riches of Christ. In the twilight of the short summer night he passed an iceberg, and was amazed to see on the top of it a dreadful-looking man with a shock of red hair. Hailing the man, and enquiring of his state, he was told that it was Judas. This one night in the year he was permitted to leave his fiery pit and cool himself on the iceberg. And this because *once* he had come across a poor leper who lay helpless on the edge of the Syrian desert with the hot sand blowing into his sores. And Judas had taken off his own cloak, and covered up the leper, before he went upon his way. What we say about this story is that it is beautiful indeed, but grotesque. It did not of course seem at all grotesque to the contemporaries of St. Brendan. Why should it? The grotesqueness is simply a matter of intellectual change : the beauty and the truth are of the things which never change. But in point of fact we have every reason to suppose that *intellectually* these Celtic saints were very much more in sympathy with our Lord's methods of teaching than we are. All life, especially all religious life, was dramatic for them ; and their religious beliefs fell quite naturally (as in this case) into a dramatic form. St. Brendan never saw Judas on the top of an iceberg, nor did Judas—as far as we can tell—ever show compassion upon a poor sufferer. But all the same the story embodies a true lesson in this dramatic way with infinitely better effect than any amount of sermons or essays, and was far better adapted to the character of that race and age. A man must be hopelessly narrow and stupid who complains of the story because it was not literally true. Dramatically it was true in the highest degree, and that is much more important and valuable for most men. Even so our Lord's story of Doom, which inculcates the same great lesson in a far more solemn way, has essentially the character of drama, not of history. One is Divine and the other is human ; but there is far more in common between them than there is between any parable of our Lord and a religious discourse of our own day.

The whole question, therefore, of the destiny of

P

the lost is open to discussion. It cannot be settled offhand by appealing to this or that saying of our Lord. When people employ themselves in the treatment of isolated passages, or the hunting up of texts, in order to support a thesis, an opinion, they do no good and they never get any further. All these controversialists, however fair and candid their method and their temper, err because they start with the assumption that our Lord and the New Testament writers *intend* to teach us a definite and harmonious doctrine about things to come. No doubt this assumption is natural enough. It has been fostered too by that habit, which was so universal in the middle ages, of treating theology as an exact science in which it was possible and proper to make the most absolute assertions on every conceivable topic of religious interest. Not to be certain about anything, not to be able to give a definite answer to any question asked, was to bring religion into contempt, and little better than confessing yourself an infidel. As a nation we have gone away from that, too far perhaps, lapsing into an utter vagueness of belief and a cold indifference to religious truth. But in *some* respects the revolt from the over-definiteness of mediæval theology is altogether justified, and can hardly be carried too far. There are subjects about which our Lord speaks indeed, and speaks very strongly, but in such a way as to baffle every attempt to take His words literally or to translate them into dogma. On these subjects — and the final destiny of the wicked is one of them—it is quite useless either

to put His language again and again through the
mill, or to supplement His authority with that of
the Church or eminent thinkers in the Church.
For neither the Church nor any member of it ever
had any source of information but what is contained
in our Lord's teaching as declared in the Gospels.
It is notorious that the current belief of the early
Church about future things was as uncertain, as
hesitating, as fluctuating, as it is now—and for the
same reason. Doubtless in the West men were
inclined to take our Lord's sayings in a more literal
sense than they were in the East; but that is a
part of the general character of the Western mind,
and we are quite alive to it.   It may be fairly
said that the tradition of the Church throws no
light at all upon those problems of the life beyond
the veil which exercise the minds of men so much.
Speculation on these subjects has been always rife
from the Shepherd of Hermas downwards.   The
author of that strange book deals with future
things quite boldly, and by means of parables and
similitudes not wholly unlike our Lord's.   But it
is as clear as day that he neither received any
authoritative guidance himself nor was able to
give any to others.   His eschatology resembles in
some respects that of modern universalism, but it
is purely speculative.   He did not influence to any
considerable extent the mind of the Church.   Nor
would it be easy to say who did influence it in
this respect.   The cross currents of opinion ran
hither and thither much as they do now, and if
they ultimately set in one direction, that was due

rather to the force of certain habits than to anything else. The habit, *e.g.*, of praying for the dead, which the first Christians took over quite naturally from the Jews, inevitably modified the ordinary beliefs of men about the present state of the departed. When to their prayers for the dead they added the offering of "the gifts" in the Eucharist, and of alms, then a great religious force came into play which led to many and unexpected developments. But these had no theological value. It is quite possible to watch the process as it came about, to see opinion concerning future things gradually settling, stiffening, hardening. But it is almost impossible not to see that these changes, these modifications, were not due to any access of light: they owed almost nothing to any general or authoritative teaching of the Church: they went on in the dark amongst the common people who knew but little even of the Gospels: they were forced on by the slow but constant pressure of the longing to be able to think, and able to say, something definite about things to come, something which could be worked in with their habits of religious devotion and observance. Even St. Augustine, *e.g.*, has no consistent doctrine of the future life, except so far as it stands in connection with his elaborated scheme of predestination and reprobation.

We have to fall back on the question whether our Lord Himself intended to teach any doctrine of the Things Beyond which can be stated with dogmatic certainty. His teaching about the Kingdom of

Heaven, here or hereafter, is almost entirely by way
of parables. A parable is for the most part fairly
plastic in the hands of those who wish to make use
of it for a purpose. It may generally be brought
with more or less success into harmony with a pre-
conceived scheme of theology. The process of
"reading in" has in fact been carried to an extraordinary length. But in the end the parables assert
their freedom. It is felt to be impossible to pin them
down to the clear-cut and nicely-balanced affirma-
tions of creeds and confessions. They are incom-
parably suggestive, impressive ; but they always
retain a large element of the mysterious, of the
inexplicable. They are pictures : they are scenes
from a drama : they have the glory of the shifting
tints which come and go upon the clouds of sunset.
Whilst they throw a flood of light upon the
principles of the Kingdom, that very light baffles
and blinds us when we strive to look into the secrets
of the future. Our Lord's pictures of things to come
are indeed, in a certain way, extraordinarily realistic.
But they are too realistic for our purpose. With
whatever regret, we have to put them away from us ;
we have to say "it is impossible to take this literally,
for it is not in harmony with His own revelation of
the Divine character and purpose : it is part of the
picture, and goes with the rest of the picture to
produce an effect and to teach a lesson which is
wonderful and true ; but it is not possible to isolate
it and turn it into a dogmatic statement." That
is what we always come to at the last. It does not
seem to be true that our Lord ever lifts the veil

which hides from us the things to come. He lifts, now and again, one or more *folds* of the veil, but never all. By means of a hundred figures, similitudes, comparisons, He intimates the nature, the character, of the life to come, and the principles on which the last Judgment will be conducted. But something of the veil is always left; there is always (even where it *seems* at first to be entirely abandoned) an element of allegory and of symbol which proves to be larger and (from one point of view) more hopeless, the longer we examine it. Finally, we are forced to believe that our Lord only taught about things to come in such a way as to throw light on the things that are. It is always and everywhere the life that now is which interests Him, which occupies Him. When His discourse is most " eschatological " and most " apocalyptic " it is still, in the reality of things, our life here and now that He is illustrating. His constant insistence upon His speedy Coming, upon the nearness of His visible Appearing, has no other object than to create for us an atmosphere of expectation, an abiding sense of living under His eye, of being within measurable distance of the final award, which is of the first necessity to us if we are to live aright. In the natural and obvious sense of His words, they have been falsified by the historic event. That does not trouble us, because we know that His words were right and true, however little we can explain them, historically. And the atmosphere of expectation which they created remains and will remain. In the life we now live the Judge *is* always before the door, always with His finger on the latch; and the "next thing" is always His appearing, His scrutiny, His award. Even that awful description of the last Assize and the doom of those on the left hand has all its true and certain reference to the life here and now. It also creates an atmosphere, not so much of expectation as of recognition. It opens our eyes to recognize our Lord and Master in the midst of us, at our doors, and at our mercy. It reveals to us with overwhelming force how much our Lord thinks of acts of kindness done here and now. If we try to make it tell us secrets of the future, then it only baffles and bewilders. It would not be difficult to go through all the other Scriptures and to show that however much they *seem* to reveal, the residuum of revelation when examined and sifted is almost *nil*. Nothing can be made of the Apocalypse in this direction. It too throws floods of light upon the life that now is and upon God's way of looking at things, but in spite of its name and form it tells us nothing certain, nothing definite, of things to come. It is a series of cloud-scapes, grand and beautiful and awful too, and no more. As a revelation of future events which can be set down in order it has long been given over as a happy hunting ground for unhappy lunatics, who take their pastime therein. Devout and instructed people know that it was given for far other and higher uses. Even so extraordinarily definite and precise a prophecy as appears in 2 Thess. ii. about the Man of Sin—from which there appears no possibility of escape—is thrown again into an utter uncertainty by St. John's assertion[1] that Antichrist was already come. Tradition has always identified Antichrist with the Man of Sin; yet St. John seems distinctly to resolve the Antichrist into a series of false and misleading teachers (or teachings rather) which had already begun to do their evil work in his day. It is quite open for us therefore to hold, *on the authority of Scripture itself,* that St. Paul's Man of Sin is only a dramatic embodiment and personification of false principles which were more or less distinctly at work in apostolic days—and much more now. So that here also, where it seemed to be out of the question, we are fetched back again for all practical purposes to our life here and now. Everywhere there is promise that our impatient curiosity about the future will be gratified. Everywhere beneath this appearance there is real and solid teaching about the present, and nothing else that is tangible. Does not our Lord intend to teach us—in His own unexpected way—that we do well to leave the future alone? It belongs to Him, and we can perfectly well trust Him with it. Heaven and Hell have, in some ways, been far too prominent in our religious systems. It is not only that the smoke of Hell has blackened the gates of Heaven, as one has put it: it is that Heaven and Hell have combined to rob our present life of the seriousness, the importance, the *all*-importance, which really belongs to it. A certain missionary hymn deplores the fact that the heathen are living "without one thought of heaven or hell." That might be even considered

---

[1] 1 John ii. 18; 2 John 7.

a blessing. What is really (and unspeakably) dreadful is, that they live without a thought of God as
their Father, of Christ as their Saviour, here and
now. It is after all only to-day that matters. If
to-day is lived aright, in God and for God, there is
no need to trouble about to-morrow—whether the
morrow which brings fresh appetite for daily food, or
the morrow which shall bring the end of all things.
It is quite safe with God anyhow. The less we trouble
about it, the less we speculate about it, the better.
" Just for to-day " is the true rule of Christian thought
as it is of Christian prayer. For all holy intents and
purposes Heaven and Hell have neither value nor
interest except as the background upon which the
present life is to be thrown up in all the intensity of
its eternal and immeasurable importance. Those
who peer with magnifying glasses into the background of the picture can scarcely appreciate or
even understand the picture itself.

This seems to be the mind of Christ as manifested
in the parables of the Kingdom, and in His doctrine
of the Future. He does not in the least avoid the
future. There are few of His parables which do not
run on even to the end of things. He does not spare
even the darkest colours, the most terrible suggestions. He magnifies in every possible way the gain
and the loss which lie in the future. But every single
thing He says has its reference to the life which now
is, *and becomes unintelligible the moment that we try
to understand it in any other way.* Again and again
we listen to Him with bated breath, we say to ourselves, " surely He is really going to tell us something

now about the actual conditions of the Future Life."
Again and again we find out, slowly and reluctantly
maybe, that He has only taught us a fresh and more
striking lesson of the life which now is. And we,
poor fools, are filled with chagrin because we really
know nothing at all about the conditions of life
beyond the grave, about the course of future events,
or the end of the world. And yet all such knowledge would be absolutely useless to us, whereas it
is "life eternal" here and now to know God the
Father and Jesus Christ whom He has sent.[1] The
parables of the Kingdom cover an extraordinary
range of picture-subjects. But the Kingdom itself
"is within you."[2]

---

[1] John xvii. 3.   [2] Luke xvii. 21.

EXCURSUS I.

ON SOME SAYINGS ABOUT THE KINGDOM OF HEAVEN

IN writing about the Kingdom of Heaven and the parables in which its many and various aspects are set forth, it is impossible to leave quite out of sight certain detached sayings which declare the nature of the Kingdom in a very trenchant way.

I. "The Kingdom of God is within you." (St. Luke xvii. 21.) That would indeed be a most pregnant and decisive utterance, if we could be sure that our Lord meant it so. Unfortunately (shall we venture to say?) we cannot take it with the unhesitating simplicity of the author of the "Imitation of Christ," because as the words stand in the Greek they are susceptible of another rendering. The Revised Version has in the margin, "The Kingdom of God is in the midst of you": and this is preferred by Dr. Plummer in his recent commentary ("International Critical: St. Luke"). As far as the grammar is concerned either translation is equally tenable, and the choice between them turns upon considerations which are fairly well balanced. The immediate context favours "in the midst of you," for our Lord was speaking to the Pharisees who expected the Kingdom to be ushered in with signs and portents, with pomp and circumstance. That, He said, was a fundamental error. It was the very nature of the Kingdom to come in quietness and without attracting

observation. Men would not be able to point the finger
at it and say "here it comes," "for, behold, the Kingdom
of God is [already] amongst you." If we take it so, we
recall at once the words of John the Baptist (St. John i.
26), "in the midst of you standeth one whom ye know
not." It is true that the two words are not identical : but
they seem to be indistinguishable in meaning. In both
cases the Jews overlooked the really important and crucial
fact because they were looking at or looking for something
more conspicuous. By the singularity of his life and
preaching John the Baptist had forced himself upon the
attention of all the people, and even of the Rulers. They
discussed the question whether he could be the Expected,
wholly oblivious of the fact that the Expected had been
for thirty years domiciled among them. So again they
discussed the signs of the promised Kingdom, and asked
our Lord's opinion about them, in total ignorance of the
fact that the Kingdom was already set up in their midst.
It was undoubtedly all part of the same fundamental and
persistent error, and it was rebuked in almost identical
words. "*He* is here ; *it* is here ; here—in the very midst
of you—if you only knew it." There is no doubt that such
is the common-sense interpretation of these memorable
words, and as such it must always command our respectful
acquiescence, if nothing more.

But there is much to be said on the other side. "The
Kingdom of God is *within* you" goes further than the
other, further than the immediate occasion required : moreover it is not addressed to the Rulers, but to mankind
at large. But all that is quite in keeping with our Lord's
manner. When, *e.g.*, our Lord exclaimed (St. John iv. 48)
"Except *ye* see signs and wonders *ye* will in no wise
believe," He was assuredly not speaking to that simple-
minded nobleman from Capernaum. Only a hopeless

stupidity will go on maintaining that. He had in His mind's eye the general mass of the Galileans who received Him because they had seen or heard of His miracles, but had no mind to accept His claims or His teachings : He saw behind them an innumerable multitude of all nations whose attitude towards the Kingdom would be equally unspiritual and unsatisfactory : and in the sorrow of His heart He spoke to them, as represented (for the moment) by the supplicant before Him. It is impossible to doubt that His words over and over again surpassed the scope and range of what was immediately present. We are justified therefore in thinking it possible, and even probable, that in answering the question of the Pharisees He gave utterance to a saying of the widest and most lasting significance. "The Kingdom of God is *within* you" : *i.e.*, its most characteristic development, its most proper and necessary manifestation, is an *inward* one— inward to the souls of men. In other words the Kingdom of God is a state of mind and soul which is reproduced in a multitude of individuals—a state which is characterized by the action of certain spiritual powers, by the dominance of certain moral and religious principles. If you want to find the Kingdom of God, our Lord would say, you need not expect to read of its advent in the daily papers, or to hear the news in the gossip of the market place : its progress will not be reported in Reuter's telegrams, nor will its shares be quoted on the Stock Exchange : it will not fall under the cognizance of parliaments, or convocations, or councils : whatever outward connections and developments it may have, these will not be of its essence, because *that* is and must be inward to the souls of men.[1] That is quite

[1] The late Dr. Frederick Field took it in this sense, adding the following apt quotation from JOHN HALES' *Golden Remains :* "Let every man retire into himself, and see if he can find this kingdom in

in our Lord's manner, and we may accept it as His meaning. If we do, there are two things to be said about it.
In the first place, it requires balancing, like everything else
which concerns the Kingdom. For however much the
Kingdom of God is within us, its manifestation will and
must pass out into life and action. We cannot help that.
We cannot really cry "hands off" to Christ in the name of
politics, *e.g.* We cannot seriously maintain that the citizen
or the official or the statesman should restrict his
Christianity entirely to his private life because the Kingdom of God is within us. It is indeed notorious that
well-meaning people allow themselves to do a thousand
things in a public capacity which they would never do as
private Christians; but it is certain that in this matter
they are self-deceived, and will suffer a rude awakening
some day. As Christians we are bound to give the most
careful and scrupulous heed to a multitude of outward
questions and considerations. But in the second place we
must never quit our grasp upon the fundamental principle
of the inwardness of the Kingdom. We are driven to
deal with the outsides of things, with tests, observances,
statistics, organizations, and so on. As far as other people
are concerned we can only get at the Kingdom from outside. And so it comes to pass that for an innumerable
number the outside becomes almost everything. They
never get beyond it: it absorbs all their interest. What
a fearful lot of arithmetic has got into the Kingdom of
Heaven, in our days! What counting of heads, what
touting for mere numbers, what adding up of figures, of
attendances, of statistics, of all kinds! "Religious
statistics" they are called, by a curious euphemism,
since no art of human nomenclature can make statistics

his heart; for if he find it not there, in vain will he find it in all the
world besides."

religious. We cannot too highly value the services which the shell renders to the nut that grows and ripens within its shelter. But if one should spend his time in gathering nut-shells, quite indifferent as to whether there was any nut inside or not, he would be exactly like some very active "religious" workers of to-day. One is indeed sometimes disposed to think that the enormous growth of religious agencies and organizations in the present age must be a bitter disappointment to the Lord of the Harvest—for there is no corresponding increase of inward religion. Increase there may be; but nothing commensurate with the immense expansion of machinery. There are indeed no outward and visible criteria of the true welfare of the Kingdom. There is a vast amount of action and reaction between the outward and visible, and the inward and invisible, but the one gives no direct clue to the other: and it is within, and out of sight, that the essential truth of the Kingdom is to be found.

II. "The Kingdom of God is not meat and drink; but righteousness and peace and joy in the Holy Ghost." (Romans xiv. 17.) That is a glorious saying, because it is so strong, so clear, so sweeping. It lays down a principle to which one may always appeal; it is a fundamental law of the Kingdom which can never be abrogated, or shelved, or made of none effect by human explanations. Exactly like the former saying of our Lord's, it needs first to be balanced, and then (in this balanced state) to be reasserted. It is obvious that St. Paul himself had a good deal to say about meat and drink—from a purely Christian standpoint. It was not open to him to dismiss such topics from his religious teaching on the ground that the Kingdom was purely spiritual. He goes so far as to intimate that it might be a Christian duty

to abstain all one's life from eating flesh or drinking wine,
if either of these things were an occasion of falling to
one's fellow-Christians. Elsewhere he shows very scant
respect for the arguments of those Corinthian Christians
who pushed his own teaching to an extreme. "The
Kingdom of God," they said, "is within us, as our
Lord taught: it is not meat or drink, as the Apostle
has told us: this outward separateness of Christians in
matters of no vital importance is a blunder: it has done
great harm to Christianity by bringing us into suspicion,
and has caused us to be plausibly accused of an anti-
social superstition: we will retain all our Christian
sentiments and principles—but we will accept invitations
to feasts held in heathen temples." So argued, so acted,
many of the Christians in Corinth. It may be said
without offence that the vast majority of British Christians,
under similar circumstances, would take the same line.
A good dinner is never to be despised. And surely a
man may have his own religion, and yet sit down to
meat with Mohammedans or heathens of any possible
kind, if they know how to behave decently. If the
"weak brother" were objected, the reply would not be
favourable to the weak brother or to his pretensions to
interfere with our liberty. It is not necessary to condemn
this attitude, although it is natural to regard it with some
apprehension. It is permissible to think that St. Paul
was convinced that *in this particular instance* the action
of the Corinthian Christians was injudicious and unfortunate. In this conviction he wrote to them with his usual
earnestness, and strength of speech. It does not follow
that he would have applied the same line of argument
to another case which on the face of it might appear
very similar. He would not, *e.g.*, have approved the
severity of Tertullian, who thought it a sinful paltering

with idolatry for Christians to decorate their front doors with laurels in honour of the Emperor's birthday. For the heathens, it appeared, associated this practice with certain idolatrous beliefs and intentions. Clearly, these questions belong to that wide borderland where we have to reconcile the claims of Christian principles which are not coincident but complemental. No Divine regulation has surveyed the watershed, or laid down the exact frontier: it is left to common sense and piety to decide in each particular case. Even St. Paul could do no more than bring his own piety and common sense to bear upon the special questions of *his* day: and even he cannot free us from the obligation to use *ours* in the questions of *our* day. Still, we cannot forget how he wrote to the Corinthians that "thus sinning against the brethren, and wounding their conscience" they sinned "against Christ." Nay, he left it at least an open question whether it was not a direct sin against God. "Do we provoke the Lord to jealousy?" he cried; "are we stronger than He?" In other words, "are we so sure of ourselves that we can afford to sail so near the wind, and to do things in the name of Christian liberty which look perilously like playing with idolatry?" Certain it is that as Christians we can never eat or drink without some distinct reference to Christ, and to our position as His servants and soldiers. But then, apart from these considerations of the moral effect it may have upon ourselves or others, there is not anything religious about eating or drinking. It is absolutely indifferent; and all the Church regulations or Church censures in the world cannot make it otherwise. In all ages people have had very strong ideas on the subject of eating and drinking, some of them sensible enough, and some very foolish: but from the point of view of the Kingdom they are

Q

equally valueless. To put it quite simply (and sometimes it is well to use great plainness of speech) God does not care in the very least what or when or how we eat or drink, so as we do not damage ourselves or others. And *He* cannot be *made* to care, and therefore *it* cannot be *made* to matter. All the old distinctions between meats were abolished for ever, when our Lord laid down the irrevocable principle of "indifference" in St. Mark vii. 14-20. "This He said, making all meats clean." But the case which best illustrates our saying is that of the "disciplinary" decree about meats made by the Council of Jerusalem (Acts xv. 29). That decree has never been revoked, and therefore there are Christians (of a careful and punctilious disposition) who regard it as binding still. They point out very truly that not only had it the highest conceivable authority, human and Divine, at the time: not only is it recorded in Holy Writ: not only has it never been revoked: but in respect of "fornication" it is certainly irrevocable, and there is no distinction made between this part of the decree and that which concerns meats. Yet the common sense of the Christian folk has long ago made it clear to them that (apart from sanitary considerations) there is no reason at all why we should abstain from things strangled or from blood. Also it is clear that if *in certain cases* we should abstain from things offered to idols it would be out of consideration for other people, and not because of this decree. Even St. Paul told his converts they might buy anything exposed for sale, without asking any questions. Now on what ground do we justify this? Simply on the ground that the Kingdom is not meat and drink, and therefore no man may judge us in meat or in drink, and therefore the Church itself cannot lay down any *permanent* rule about meat or drink. It would be *ultra vires*, because it would contradict our Lord's principle of "indifference." Only to meet a *present* emergency, and for *present* edification, may the Church lay down rules about food; and as fast as the special circumstances change, these rules become obsolete. They need no revoking; they fade away of themselves, because they are only upheld by some stress of necessity, or some present demand of charity, against the fundamental and permanent law of "indifference." All rules of fasting must ultimately fall under the same head. It is certainly within the power of the Church to make rules of fasting; but these require to be continually revived and re-enacted either by the express voice of the Church or by the general consensus of her children. Otherwise they too fade away, and lose their binding power. We cannot make it otherwise, because the nature of the case does not permit of anything more permanent. The Kingdom of God *is* righteousness and peace and joy—and therefore it excludes the sins of the flesh for ever. It *is not* meat and drink—and therefore it can only allow of rules for present edification in respect of eating or drinking or fasting.

III. "It is hard for a rich man to enter into the Kingdom of Heaven" (St. Matt. xix. 23). To which He added the tremendously strong assertion that it was easier for a camel to go through a needle's eye than for a rich man to enter into the Kingdom of God. Of course we have nothing to do here with that imaginary gate called "the needle's eye" through which no camel could pass without being unloaded. That gate is a product (and a monument) of Western stupidity in dealing with our Lord's words.[1] It was simply a very ordinary proverbial saying to express what we should call "perfectly im-

[1] See WRIGHT's *Some New Testament Problems*, pp. 125-133.

possible." It is obvious that what is "perfectly impossible" in the common mind and speech of men, does in fact often come to pass. Much more in the Kingdom, where miracles are always happening. The real difficulty with us is not in the strength of our Lord's language, but in the assertion which He made. We cannot honestly say that being rich is any particular hindrance to a man's private religion. It exposes him, no doubt, to some temptations; but it saves him from others. It does not seem possible to believe that this saying expresses a permanent feature of the Kingdom if we treat entering into the Kingdom as equivalent to being "saved," or being justified by faith. It is universally taught at any rate that a rich man may be a good Christian, and die in the Lord, without devoting more than a small percentage of his wealth to good works. It is certain that rich men very often wish to enter the Kingdom, and not infrequently lead exemplary lives. It would seem very harsh to assert that their Christianity has no reality about it, and will avail them nought. Yet here is our Lord's saying, which appears to contradict this testimony of experience. It is a great perplexity. There is however one sense of the words in which they have been abundantly confirmed (and unexpectedly too) by the history of the Kingdom. There is no reason that we can see why a rich man should not enter the Kingdom *as a believer* just as well as a poor man: and in fact he does. But as long as the world lasts he will never enter the Kingdom as a fellow labourer with God. It may sound startling, but it is nevertheless true that the possession of riches is an absolute disqualification for success in the ministry of the Gospel. The enormous majority of mankind are poor. To the poor the Gospel is preached. Between the poor and the rich there is a great gulf fixed which the best intentions, the most kindly feelings, cannot

pass for religious purposes. The poor are quite accessible
to the gifts of the rich, and in certain ways amenable to
their counsel and influence—but not in religion. In this
they will in fact only listen to their brethren who know
by experience their sorrows, their wants, their weakness,
who share the narrowness and sadness of their lot; not
to those who stand afar off and try to get at them with
good words from their vantage ground of comfort and
luxury. Many things tend to conceal this great truth from
our eyes—but it *is* a truth. All religious history bears
it out. The Incarnation itself meant that our Lord
emptied Himself of all His own proper glories and
immunities and prerogatives, and put Himself down on
a level (as far as outward things were concerned) with the
poor of the flock, with the mass of the people. They
would not have listened to Him as they did if He had
lived in a fine house, attended by many servants, and
surrounded by unusual comforts. Perhaps His poverty
has been exaggerated in popular teaching. That does
not alter the fact that He threw in His lot unequivocally
with the poor, as distinguished from the rich. And it
does seem strange that those whose great desire is to
preach the religion of the Incarnation should have failed
to grasp its most obvious lesson. To become poor—in
other words to forego all the comforts and indulgences
which belong to the well-to-do classes—is an essential
condition for acquiring spiritual influence over the mass
of men. This was true of our Lord, was true of the
Apostles, was true of the early and the mediæval Christian
missionaries, was true of the Friars, was true of the Anabaptist teachers, is true of the Salvation Army. The
rich man may have influence in the world (though even
there far less than is supposed): he may have influence
in the Church, regarded as an outward and visible organi-

zation; but in the Kingdom of Heaven, regarded as the Empire of Christ over men's hearts and lives, he has next to none; the mere fact of his being rich for ever debars him from getting close to his fellow men and speaking to their hearts. "To the poor the Gospel is preached," our Lord declared; and He might have added (for He left it in no manner of doubt) "by the poor." As far as one's own salvation is concerned voluntary poverty seems to be a counsel of perfection in the Kingdom; but as far as other people's is concerned, it is a condition precedent. It may be that this is what our Lord chiefly had in view in those extremely strong sayings of His about the unfortunate results of being rich. For did He not habitually regard men, not merely as having souls to be saved, but as having gifts and capacities to be used in His service?

IV. "Whosoever shall not receive the Kingdom of God as a little child, he shall in no wise enter therein" (St. Mark x. 15). We have already considered the saying that "of such is the Kingdom of Heaven." We have found it the only really available Scriptural argument for the baptism of infants. Other arguments there are, of course, but they are either indirect and precarious, or else they are neutralized by other considerations of a similar character and scope. But this one seems overwhelming. If infants are so dear to our Lord; if the Kingdom of Heaven is exactly suited for them, and they for it; how is it possible to refuse them baptism? The visible Church is not indeed the Kingdom of Heaven, but it corresponds to it—and the more closely it corresponds the better. How should we exclude from the visible Church those who are freely welcomed to the Kingdom? No means of admission to the Church has

ever been known but baptism. Granted all the difficulties ;
granted that in other respects the argument is indecisive ;
our Lord's words about the children and the Kingdom
will always settle the question for the great mass of
Christians.

But it is not the privileges of the children, but the
character of the Kingdom, which we have now to consider.
What was it which appeared to our Lord so admirable and
so necessary in the childlike mind that He barred the
Kingdom to any other? It could not have been the
innocency of childhood—which is to us so great a part of
its charm—because He flung the gates of the Kingdom
wide open to the penitent. If we think of simplicity, of
guilelessness, of openness, we shall no doubt have got
somewhere near the point we want to reach. In doing
this we recognize instantaneously a type of character which
is difficult—if not impossible—to cultivate. No one ever
exhorted other people to have this childlike mind. He
might as well urge upon them to have blue eyes. Doubtless if you have it, it is charming ; but if not, what can you
do? All men and all nations—and, to a great extent, all
ages—have the defects of their virtues. The virtues of
modern, civilized, Western life are many and great and
admirable : but the defects which go along with them are
(generally speaking) fatal to anything childlike. We are
much more likely to meet with *this* in a backward and
unsuccessful community. This is part of that general
balance of advantage which is no doubt so much more of
a fact than we are willing to admit. We are filled with
pity and horror when we think of the evil conditions under
which other people in other lands (or even our own) have
had to spend their lives, or have to now. Yet in some
ways their manner of life has been more conducive to the
traits and tempers loved of Christ. This childlike temper,

e.g., which is so rare among the most representative classes of our own people, is declared to be necessary for entrance into the Kingdom. Nothing at any rate which contradicts it can permanently remain in the Kingdom. It is an essential element in personal religion. There is therefore nothing more to be said save that this declaration of our Lord's, like that other one about the rich man, is very disquieting. Over against our modern life stands our Lord in an attitude of sternness which is distinctly embarrassing. We do so want to be on good terms with everybody, and especially with Him. Moreover He has been always represented to us in such a gracious and attractive light. It has been a foregone conclusion with us that amongst the enormous advantages of our modern life was this,—that we were at perfect liberty without let or hindrance to serve Him in a quiet and sensible way. Now it appears that however attractive He is to us, our modern life is not at all attractive to Him. He looks upon it coldly : speaks of it almost harshly. The evils of His own age, which He for the most part took for granted, have very largely disappeared. But the virtues which He demanded, on which He insisted with so great emphasis, are exactly those which seem to flourish least in our own age and land. It is— when one is willing to lay all pretences aside and to look it fairly in the face—very disquieting. One can only conclude that our Lord never intended it to be anything else.

It is not of course pretended that these are all the sayings about the Kingdom which need to be carefully considered. Far from it. But they are perhaps the ones of most outstanding importance. They declare fundamental truths which men are constantly engaged in explaining away, constantly tempted to ignore. Nevertheless they remain, and will always have to be reckoned with. No ingenuity of argument or deduction, no seeming cogency or clearness in the great art of putting things, can ever make any part of our Lord's teaching about the Kingdom less infallibly true. These principles—like the law of the Medes and Persians, but for an infinitely better reason—cannot be changed.

EXCURSUS II.

ON SUFFERING AS A NOTE OF THE KINGDOM OF HEAVEN

THAT suffering *is* in a very marked degree characteristic of the Kingdom is of course a fact which lies beyond dispute. When the first missionaries impressed it upon their converts "that through many tribulations we must enter into the Kingdom of God," they did but re-echo and reinforce out of their own actual experience the repeated declarations of our Lord. "In the world ye shall have tribulation" was not an isolated warning : He had uniformly asserted, or assumed, the same thing. The life-long experience of the Apostles left no doubt upon their minds that the law of suffering was general and permanent. "All that would live godly in Christ Jesus shall suffer persecution," says St. Paul in his latest writing ; and he betrays no consciousness of the tremendously sweeping and unqualified character of the assertion. Similarly St. John at a still later date writes to his fellow Christians as their brother and companion "in the tribulation and Kingdom and patience which are in Jesus." Nothing could be more simply effective than the position of the "Kingdom" in this sentence. It is identified by the mere arrangement of the words with persecution from without, with patient endurance from within. It is one of the unsolved problems of Christianity how this unhesitating expectation came to be falsified in fact, and why (since it was to be falsified) it was permitted to express itself so strongly in Holy Scripture. People gloss over the difficulty by pointing out that all who wish to be good and consistent Christians must be prepared to meet with annoyance and ridicule, and even some measure of petty persecution. They ignore the fact that these things are obviously *not* the persecutions or the tribulations spoken of in Scripture, and that even these are escaped by a very large proportion of Christians. A man who is determined to be honest and to act upon his principles will have to pay a certain price whatever his religion (or want of religion) may be. Quâ Christian, however, it does not seem that he really has anything to suffer — except of course in the Turkish Empire, and in a few other dark places of the earth. St. Paul therefore was mistaken, or at any rate he gave a more unlimited and unqualified expression to his conviction than the event has justified. The vast majority of Christian people may live as close to the teaching of their Master as they please —or as they find otherwise possible — without incurring any particular ill-will, or suffering any persecution worth speaking of.

But what is chiefly of importance from our present point of view is this, that the future glories and heavenly rewards of the Kingdom are uniformly connected in Scripture with the endurance of persecution and tribulation in this life. Take such a favourite and familiar passage as the latter half of the seventh chapter of the Revelation. What comfort, what joy, what a blessed foretaste of good things to come has not that passage afforded to Christian people! How the words set themselves to music, the most tender, the most moving, the most triumphant too! The music which has died upon the ear in some cathedral church in cadences of incomparable sweetness, lives for ever in the soul. And always it repeats itself, with a sudden thrill of great joy, when life is weary, and the heart is sick and sore. "They shall hunger no more . . . neither thirst any more . . . neither shall the sun light on them, nor any heat . . . the Lamb which is in the midst of the Throne shall feed them . . . shall lead them unto living fountains of water . . . God shall wipe away every tear from their eyes." By how many dying beds have we read these words, and dying lips have moved responsive to them, and faded eyes have shone for a moment with the new light of that hope which is full of immortality. Does it not seem cruel, intolerable, to suggest to these good and gentle souls, whose hope is in Christ, that they have no right whatever to these words? Yet what can we say, honestly? "These are they which came out of the great tribulation." That is what the "Elder" told St. John, and it is impossible for us to dispute it. If he did not know, no one else could. It is equally impossible to pretend that the good people whose dying hours are soothed to-day with these Scriptures have come out of the great tribulation. As a rule they have had no tribulation worth speaking of, and certainly not that of which the Elder spake. They have washed their robes (mystically) in the blood of the Lamb. Be it so. But as they have not come through the great tribulation, it is sheer dishonesty to affect that the vision pertains to them. No doubt "sheer dishonesty" is a hard expression to use: but the use of it is justified. We have got into the habit, and the habit has become inveterate and universal, of taking Scriptures which apply only to martyrs and appropriating them to all Christians who have lived decent lives or died anything like edifying deaths. It is no doubt very agreeable, very consolatory, but it is dishonest.

It may seem an extreme thing to say, but it is not far from the truth, that in the whole New Testament there is no intimation of the future destiny of those believers who have not suffered for and with their Lord, *i.e.* of the vast majority of Christians nowadays. They will of course be "saved"—for "whosoever shall call upon the name of the Lord shall be saved." But we are not told anything about their state. "If we suffer, we shall also reign with Him" is the law which is always expressed or implied in all New Testament references to the glory which shall be revealed. "No cross, no crown" expresses well enough this law, which is yet so strangely ignored. For countless Christian people look to be crowned, who have never had any cross to bear. Perhaps they have regarded the common ills of life—such as they would have had in any case to bear — as their cross. But there is no authority for this in the New Testament. It is everywhere represented that our Lord's disciples would meet with trial and suffering peculiar to themselves; and the patient endurance of such trial and suffering is made the basis and condition of their heavenly reward. Most of all, of course, is this the case in that strange book of Revelation, whence we draw almost all our pictures and our popular ideas of Heaven. It is emphatically a book of martyrs. It is penetrated through and through with the pungent reek from those living torches in the gardens of Nero. Whatever doubts exist about the date of the Apocalypse, the internal evidence is overwhelming that it is dominated by the fiendish cruelty of Nero; by the loathing which he inspired as the arch-persecutor of Christians; by the mingled intensity of horror, of pity, of love, of triumph, with which the author contemplated the awful sufferings—*so* awful, and yet *so* glorious—of those Christians. It is quite possible that all this intensity of feeling came back to him (in some state of "ecstasy" perhaps) long after, in the isle of Patmos. But anyhow it is the horror of Nero that broods like a foul and darksome mist over the book of the Revelation   Upon the upper surface of that cloud, ugly and angry as it is in itself, the Light of God plays with effects most beautiful, most ravishing.   Out of the rainbow hues which the inspired writer there beholds he paints the scenery of that Heaven to which his fellow-sufferers have gone. It is the martyrs' Heaven, and they whom we see in that happy place have come out of "the fiery trial," "the great tribulation."   If any others are there, no mention is made of them.   Most distinctly is this the case with that phase of the Kingdom, commonly spoken of as the Millennium, which is declared unto us in Rev. xx. 4-6. There seems no good reason for refusing to accept that declaration literally, according to the common belief of the earliest Christian ages.   But there is every reason for refusing to accept the current teaching about the Millennium which finds favour with many excellent people to-day.   That teaching insists (quite fairly) on the literal acceptation of the reigning with Christ, and for a thousand years.   But it deliberately and flatly ignores the limitation expressed—and expressed as clearly as words can do it— in the crucial word "beheaded."   The word itself is a peculiar one which St. John perhaps coined — just as "guillotined" and (quite recently) "macheted" have been coined—to signify death by a certain instrument of death. It does not appear at all likely that anyone was actually killed with the old Roman "axe" (the word here used) in the Apostles' days.   Certainly the Neronian martyrs were not, as a rule.   But the "axe" was the symbol of the "terrors of the law"—the law of the Roman state— and the horror of the situation for the Christians was this, that however they were slain, by the fiendish ingenuity of the Emperor, or by the brutal violence of the mob, they were still regarded and represented as social outlaws, as public enemies, as under the ban and the wrath of that State which was fast absorbing into itself all the powers and dignities of heaven as well as of earth. The deified State, represented by the "divine" Cæsar, held the "axe" of the old Republic for ever suspended over the necks of the accursed Nazarenes. However therefore they perished in fact, in theory they were "beheaded," and St. John accurately represents the case by using the word here. There is reason then for extending the Millennial reign to all the martyrs. There is no reason, but an impudent determination to make what you please of the Word of God, for extending it to amiable and easy-going people who have never suffered anything at all for the Kingdom of Heaven's sake. It is not very reverent to dismiss the vision as being without assignable meaning. But it is much more irreverent to pretend to accept it as it stands, and then to alter its terms in favour of ourselves. St. John contemplated the *souls of the martyrs* — of those who actually died for professing a religion forbidden by the Roman State—and he contemplated nobody else. It is not possible (unless the Apostle was strangely deceived or used extremely misleading language) for any Christian of the present generation to share in the first resurrection. He cannot be beheaded for the testimony of Jesus (unless possibly he be an Armenian); he cannot make himself a public enemy by refusing to share the rites or to accept the certificates of an established idolatry.

That is no doubt an extreme instance of the way in which good people will play fast and loose with the sayings and promises of Scripture. But the practice itself is widespread and deep-rooted. It is necessary to revise all that we have so easily accepted about the future state of the saved, as well as of the lost. In both cases we have been far too ready to accept definite conclusions, and then to fortify them with passages of Scripture which do not really apply. That the future state of all who with any sincerity "call upon the name of the Lord" and "believe in the Lord Jesus Christ" will be safe and happy, we need not for a moment doubt. *But there is extremely little said about it in the New Testament.* All the great and glowing promises are for the martyrs, or at least for such as have really suffered for and with Christ. Our Lord Himself, it may be said, and the sacred writers, do not contemplate any alternative to suffering— except apostasy. Apparently it is so. But it leaves us without information regarding the future of those whose Christianity costs them nothing. To claim for them the glories and rewards of sufferers and martyrs is in the highest degree precarious.

EXCURSUS III.

ON THE DESTINY OF THE LOST

THIS is a subject which is only negatively connected with the Kingdom of Heaven. We might omit it altogether; and in view of the apparent hopelessness of making anything of it, it might seem best to do so. But no one who believes in the Kingdom of Heaven as representing God's eternal purposes for His human children can put away the question whether it is to exclude, finally and absolutely, a more or less large proportion of the human race. In all things which imply struggle, effort, failure—as the Kingdom in our Lord's teaching undoubtedly does—we are forced to ask ourselves what is to be done with those that fail. We see at once that difficulty is not only the test but the condition of excellence—human nature being what it is. But we see as clearly that difficulty involves defeat of many (we being what we are), and that the glorious result is inevitably purchased at a great price. It is quite open to us to repudiate the common idea that this life of ours was intended to be "a probation"—as though God employed Himself in putting His children through a series of tests just to see whether they could stand them or not. It is quite open to us to insist that life is "an education" of which the sole purpose and intention is training for something higher. That does not alter the fact that a countless multitude of people break down under the educational process, and are morally the worse for it. It *must* be the merest affectation to deny that Judas was only one of very many of whom we are bound to say that it is a great pity they were ever born. In saying that we do not prejudge their fate: we have in fact nothing to do with it: we know what they *are*, how degraded, how malignant, how justly called devils and children of the devil by our Lord Himself and His Apostles: and in view of what they *are*, we are compelled to regret that they were ever born. It is indeed possible to regard mankind at large with complacency. It is only possible however on two conditions: first, that exceptional advantages of circumstance place us beyond the reach of human injustice or cruelty: second, that we do not concern ourselves with the moral character of individuals. These conditions are not recognized in the Kingdom of Heaven, and therefore from the point of view of the Kingdom we are compelled to see things in a light which is always serious and often sombre. We are forced sooner or later to contemplate the destiny of those who fail, morally. How many they are, what proportion they bear to the others, is a matter so obscure that it is useless to enquire into it. No doubt many sayings of our Lord would lead us to the saddest of conclusions if we took them by themselves. On the other hand, what may be called "official" opinion in the Church has been as a rule optimistic. The obvious fact is that there are very strong reasons, very grave considerations, to be urged on either side. Practically, it depends upon the general bent and complexion of a man's mind which set of considerations appeals to him most and therefore determines his conclusion—if indeed he ever comes to any. It is enough to say that a possibility, and something more than a possibility, of failure is contemplated throughout the New

Testament. There will be those who are justly spoken of as "lost": what is to become of them? The answer to this question, which we find ourselves entirely unable to put away from us, has seemed very simple to the great majority of Christian folk. They have taken our Lord's language concerning the lost quite literally and it has left them no room for uncertainty. There is no doubt whatever that He habitually depicted their fate in the gloomiest colours possible, and in language deliberately designed to arouse the most poignant feelings of sorrow and of horror. Whatever else is false, the complacency with which the fate of the wicked is regarded by very many Christians is clearly false, because it is totally inconsistent with the *tone* in which our Lord habitually spoke. Unless the fate of the lost were (within His knowledge of it) a very frightful one, He could not have used the sort of language about it which He did use. But on the other hand we have found the gravest reasons for hesitating to take our Lord's language literally. We perceive that He habitually employed picture language, and that every attempt to read that language as if it were the ordinary prose of modern and Western life leads straight into confusion and error. The element of picture and parable in His teaching is constantly turning out to be more extensive than we had supposed. Even such a parable as that of the sheep and goats—which has always been treated as a plain declaration of what is going to happen—proves to be a parable throughout. As a picture of Judgment to come it stands no doubt in a certain relation to the facts as they shall be—but what the relation is no man can say. As the parable stands the "wicked" are absolutely identified with those that fail to show kindness to the necessitous. No such identification is possible in real life, or ever will be.

We are obliged to conclude that we have here a glorification of "love" as the greatest of Christian virtues—a
glorification which owes its peculiar form to the choice
(or necessity) which did in fact impel our Lord ever to
speak to the world in parables. According to His real
meaning it was not "the wicked" who were to go into
everlasting fire, but the want of charity which ruins so
many characters admirable enough in some other ways.
When theologians assume that "the cursed" of St. Matthew
xxv. 41 are the same people whom they habitually speak
of as "the lost" or "the wicked," they do disgraceful
violence to our Lord's teaching. If we began to divide
mankind—as our Lord does here—into those who show
kindness and those who do not, we should get two sets
of people indeed, but two sets which no theologian on
earth would ever recognize as representing the saved and
the lost. It is therefore quite illegitimate to press such
a text as St. Matthew xxv. 46 as asserting the eternity
of punishment. Those who treat the Bible mechanically
as a repertory of texts will continue to quote it in this
sense—but it will remain utterly unconvincing for those
who have considered with reverence and intelligence our
Lord's methods of teaching. He never spoke of the
destiny of the lost except in picture language, evidently
intended to produce the strongest impression of fear and
sorrow on our minds, but as evidently *not* intended to
be turned into dogmatic assertions. On this dread
subject the whole effect of His teaching is gloomy in
the extreme; but it is not definite, and cannot be made
so by any possible ingenuity in the marshalling and
handling of texts.

Against the language of our Lord is often pitted the
language of St. Paul in a few well-known places where he
glories in the expectation of a final restoration of all in-

telligent beings to their proper place in that great order of things of which Christ is the Head, and Christ the bond of union. Of this language also we must say that it is too rhetorical to be forced into the rigid form of dogmatic assertion. It points of course to a certain and glorious truth; but that truth is not so definite in all its outlines that we can assert it to be incompatible with final and irretrievable loss for some. Rather we remember that it is entirely the way of the sacred writers, and notably of our Lord, to take up some important truth and to insist upon it as if it were the only truth in existence—whereas in fact it is only one of two or more complemental truths which profoundly limit and modify one another. No "reconciliation" of these complemental truths is ever attempted, and generally speaking it is impossible. It lies beyond the reach of the human intellect and is as inaccessible as it is certain. All we can do is so to accept each as not to deny the others. To be consistent, to be logical, would be to involve oneself in the most frightful errors, and to commit oneself to the most impossible conclusions. Even in the metaphysic of the schools, if we persist in running our thoughts to earth, we come continually to a point where we *must* take one of two roads, and *each* of them leads to a blank absurdity. Much more in heavenly things, into which there enters constantly the eternal and divine, the attempt to build up logically consistent systems is beset with dangers. The truths presented to us with so much ardour of conviction, with such a vivid picturesqueness of illustration, are most certain and most necessary each in its own place; but as for harmonizing them one with another, that is only partially within our powers. In religion, as in philosophy, we are constantly confronted with alternative assertions, neither of which is tenable, yet both of which can be shown to be certain. If our Lord chose to teach in this way, it was because He had respect at once to the limitations of our minds and the needs of our souls. For practical purposes we need to grasp clearly and strongly the various truths which lie nearest to us, which are to influence our doings and shape our characters. With the ultimate synthesis of these truths He did not concern Himself; and if *we* concern ourselves, it must be with the greatest modesty and caution, and with a profound distrust of the short and easy methods of ordinary argument and reasoning.

So far, then, we have only reached this negative conclusion, that an examination of texts leads to no certain results upon the subject of the destiny of the wicked. All we can say is that the picture-language used by our Lord leaves the most gloomy impression upon our minds—an impression which is only faintly relieved by the "universalism" of certain passages in St. Paul's Epistles. But it is idle to suppose that men's convictions on such a subject will be formed by consideration of texts only. Behind all texts, and all teachings of Scripture, lie two things—the revealed character of God, and the revealed character of man. The ultimate issues of life and death, in their nature, intensity, and duration, must be decided by these. It is impossible to leave them out of sight—and yet it is difficult to introduce them without their lending themselves to wild and sweeping assertions which have no value. If we are to do any good at all we must be constantly on our guard against this danger.

Let us see first what the revealed character of man has to say to the doctrine of eternal punishment. We might have expected that since man was obviously made to be happy his whole nature would cry out against such a doctrine. But it is not so. For what we are most universally conscious of is the fact of our free will, the fact that for all permanent purposes we make ourselves what we are. That all men go to their "own place," that we shall reap just what we have sown, that we shall receive the things done in the flesh, whether good or bad—all this teaching of the New Testament commends itself absolutely to the general conscience. It may be confused with much talk about circumstance, temptation, heredity: and men expect that such things (whatever they are worth) will be allowed for: but they are profoundly convinced that they are free agents, and that they are themselves the architects and arbiters of their own future destinies. If this faith cannot be logically reconciled with the Omnipotence or Predestination of God, or with our own absolute dependence upon His free grace for anything good, that does not trouble us. A truth is not less true because it cannot be logically reconciled with others. And this truth of man's free will, and free choice, is so continually present in Scripture as the tacitly assumed basis upon which God's dealings with man, and God's sayings to man, are founded, that the two must stand or fall together. If man is not free, if he does not hold (as it were) his future in his own hands, it is not worth while to give another thought to the Scripture or to religion. But man's freedom of choice, taken by itself, makes for the irretrievable character of his loss, if he is lost at all. All experience points to the conclusion that what we designedly fling away or deliberately forfeit we can never have again. Seldom indeed is a second chance given to us in adult life. Moreover, since it is a question not of what we shall *have*, but of what we shall *be*, it is clear that the matter cannot be settled *for* us —not even by God Himself. It is not necessary to enquire whether He *could* make a bad man good in spite of himself; it is enough to say that He will not. But if a man will not seek God or do good while he is here, what possible reason is there for supposing he will do so anywhere else? The discipline of suffering may be brought to bear upon him with more severity certainly. But on the one hand that would easily become a form of compulsion—which cannot be contemplated: and on the other the bitterest sufferings here have often no good effect at all upon the sufferers. Anyhow, if we agree that things will somehow be so arranged for the wicked that they will all become good sooner or later, we seem necessarily to impart to this life an aspect of uselessness and unreality which is very hard to reconcile with the whole tone of Scripture, and with the atoning Death "under Pontius Pilate." For that Death so emphatically belonged to this world and this life that, if the spiritual probation of man is to be extended indefinitely into other worlds and other lives, it would seem as if He must suffer in all those other worlds as well as this. And that was apparently one of the speculations of Origen, which so far has not recommended itself to the Christian people. Inasmuch then as men are so generally and so obstinately convinced of their own freedom and responsibility of choice, they will (however unwillingly) incline to believe that the consequences of a life wilfully evil must be unalterable and endless. Nature and human nature do emphatically bear out the statement that what a man has sown *that* (and nothing else) he must reap : nor is there any reason to believe that even after this miserable experience he will want to sow anything else—except under compulsion.

The only alternative seems to be to suppose that God will go on making it easier and easier to do right, and more and more difficult to do wrong, until it reaches a point at which the human will is overmastered. Without arguing the matter, it is enough to say that such a thought does not harmonize with our other thoughts about God's governance of the world: it seems altogether unworthy of Him.

We have to do however with something more important even than human nature. We have to take God Himself into account. It is the great fault, the fatal weakness, of the most learned and painstaking investigations into this subject that they have left God out. In a book so able, and in some respects so fearless, as Principal Salmond's *Immortality* the whole argument (as concerns our present topic) is vitiated by this extraordinary omission. Every text bearing upon the fate of the lost is discussed with learning and candour. About the fact that God is revealed in the New Testament as our Father not a word is said. It is apparently regarded as having no bearing upon the question. Yet the destinies of the lost must be as absolutely dependent upon the will of God as those of the saved. At every moment of the eternal future whatever any living creature suffers it must suffer by the deliberate counsel and decree of the Almighty—it must owe to Him from moment to moment the very ability to suffer. There would be no difficulty in this thought if He were such a God as the Moslems acknowledge, in whom love and mercy are strictly (and indeed narrowly) limited and subordinate qualities. The God and Father of our Lord Jesus Christ is revealed to us as a God of love, as a God who *is* love, as *our* Father too. Our Lord teaches us to argue with all boldness and confidence from what we are as fathers to what God is as Father. He teaches us to scout the notion that we could be more kind, more tender-hearted, towards our children than He is towards us. "How much more" is the law of what we may expect from His fatherly goodness. It appears indeed that whatever love a father has for his children is only a derivative from, a reflexion

of, the love of the Eternal Father for us. From Him
"every family"—every collection of human beings in
which a father's influence and a father's love has any
place—gets its name in heaven and earth. In other
words, God is not revealed as Father because His relation
to us bears a certain resemblance to the fatherly relation
amongst ourselves. That is far below the truth. Whatsoever has any thought or character of fatherhood (or
fatherliness) about it among men is a faint and feeble
counterpart of the perfect and eternal Fatherhood of
God. God's Fatherhood is the original; every other,
wheresoever it may be found, is only a copy.

Since that is so—and that it *is* so is the primary revelation of the New Testament, which must needs dominate
every other—it must surely be the merest pedantry to
affect to ignore it when we discuss the destiny of the
lost. In speaking of the lost we are speaking of lost
children, and of what they will endure by the will of
their Father in Heaven. What does that fact involve?
One thing it involves certainly and absolutely, viz., that
God will never cease to love (as only He can love) every
soul which He has created in His own image and likeness.
On this point no good person ought to have the smallest
doubt, because his own heart testifies with unhesitating
assurance that it *is* so. "If ye being evil"—is there any
point in that argument? If there is—if it is legitimate
at all—it renders it impossible to suppose that the Father
who has loved such an one (prodigal though he were) up
to the moment of his death, from that moment ceases to
care for him. How could such a thought have entered
into anyone's mind? "Which of you," surely our Saviour
would say, "being a father could ever cease to love his
own child, were that child ever so wicked, so obdurate, so
lost?" Nor can anyone answer that simplest of appeals.

None of us could. Whatever else happened, whatever else might seem right and necessary, no father (worthy of the name) could ever cease to love son or daughter, present or absent, alive or dead. Wickedness does not kill love, although it may mingle with it indignation and abhorrence. Misery only adds to it a boundless pity. That is indeed fully recognized as far as this life is concerned. With the parable of the prodigal son, and its companion - stories, to help us, we preach most unrestrainedly the love of the Father towards all sinners up to the moment that they die. After that the love is supposed to change into hate, or at least into indifference. But why? Granted that their state then becomes fixed and unalterable, what has that to do with it? A father does not give up loving his prodigal son because that son has been sentenced to penal servitude for life. On the contrary, the very thought of his irremediable misery will add a greater tenderness of pity to his fatherly affection. Even supposing the man could change, and grow weary of loving one unworthy, this is not possible with God. He *is* love, and He cannot change. Our changes do not affect Him. No one has ever suggested that He loves us because we are good, or worthy of His regard, or likely to do Him credit. He loves us because He is love, and because He is our Father. There is absolutely nothing in the death of a sinner to make any difference to His love. If we were to estimate the love of God by the popular conception of it, we should have to conclude that He only loved his children as long as there was a "chance" of their becoming accessible to His love and profiting by it. That would be below the level of man's love. We do not cease to love the children who are (as far as we can see) hopelessly alienated, or even dead. As long as they are believed to exist, and to be in want or darkness, we love them without respect to what may or may not be possible in the future. We must therefore utterly and finally reject the notion that God hates the lost, or regards them with indifference, or forgets them. There is a famous sermon, said to be one of the finest in the English language, which depicts the fate of a lost soul utterly forgotten of God. It is little better than a blasphemy to suggest that God can ever forget one of His own children whom He has called into existence, whom He has pursued so many years with a divine love and patience. Imagine the earthly father that could do this thing! For a long time he has kept his heart and his door open to this prodigal son: he has sent him messages of love and kindness: he has exhausted all methods to win him back. And then the son is cast into a dungeon without hope of release. "I shall forget him," says the father: and henceforth he eats, drinks, and is merry, and not a thought of the unhappy sufferer troubles his enjoyment by day, his rest by night. Can anyone believe that the love of God is so poor a thing as this, so much below the level of human love?

What shall we say then of the wrath of God which is revealed from heaven against all ungodliness and unrighteousness of men—which abideth upon him that obeyeth not the Son? We may at least say this, that "the wrath of God" cannot possibly resemble that dark and disturbing passion of anger which is so familiar to ourselves, and which is directed against the individuals who have made us angry. That God in His holiness must of necessity be an adversary unto us as long as we do amiss is certain. And the hopeless contrariety in which the sinner finds himself as towards God, involving as it does the dreadful weight of the Divine displeasure, is spoken of by a most natural figure of speech as "the wrath of God." But it is nowhere suggested that God *is* wrath in the same sense that God *is* love. In an earthly father the keenest sense of right and wrong, the utmost detestation of iniquity, does not quench his love for his children, does not make it less. As he does not love his child for the reason that the child is good, so he does not cease to love him for the reason that he is evil. If we are to believe that God does not love the lost, we must give up the whole revelation of the Fatherhood of God as a thing which has no solid meaning and no real comfort in it. If on the other hand we believe our Lord teaching us to argue from our own hearts to His, we shall be certain that, whatever becomes of the lost, God will always love them and always (if we may say so reverently) do His best for them.

As He *is*, unchangeably and essentially, love, He will be love on earth, love in Heaven, and not less love in hell. "If I go down to hell, thou art there also," and if He is there, He will be Himself, He will be love, He will be the Father. However His manifestations of Himself may differ (for love is compatible with any degree of severity) He cannot be different *Himself*. Essentially and unchangeably He must be as much "love" towards the lowest soul in hell as towards the highest soul in Heaven— and that for ever, since there can be no variation with Him, neither shadow that is cast by turning.

So much then we have gained which is positive and unalterable. God will always love these lost souls, for whom He gave His Son to die, and will always seek their good. There are not any vindictive punishments with Him. All that is an evil dream. The fate of the wicked may be one of unspeakable misery, it may have no end visible to the human eye—but the misery will be of their own earning, not of His inflicting. The hell in which they find themselves will be the best place for them, and the least intolerable, they being what they are. The Fatherhood of God, and the fact that He is love, make this certain.

But while we can go so far—and it is an unspeakable relief to do so—we cannot go any further. There is a strong popular impression that since God loves us as a Father, He must be able and willing to make it all right for everybody. Why should anyone be unhappy under His sway of infinite love and power? Alas, a father's love on earth can do little enough towards making his children happy. They take their destinies into their own hands, and (as often as not) make themselves miserable.

It is not easy to see how it *can* be the case, but to all appearance it *is* the case, that the Almighty in imparting to us His own divine possession of moral freedom has tied His own hands as far as our happiness is concerned. We can only be happy, if good : whether we are good or not depends in great measure not on Him but on ourselves. It is true that theologians as a rule would demur to this statement. They feel bound to safeguard the absolute sovranty of God by some form of words which conceals the real issue. But the common sense of religion accepts the truth as we have stated it. It is the will of God that all men should be saved. Of course it is, for He is the Father of all. If all men are not in fact saved—if on the contrary very many are lost—that is because it depends only partially upon the will of God. Very largely it depends upon our own will, and our own will is often enough not to be saved. It is not His love that is limited, but His power. There is no other possible explanation of the facts, and this explanation of them is tacitly assumed throughout the Bible; "why *will* ye die, O house of Israel?"

It is useless therefore to suppose that because God is good, men need not fear the pains of hell. It is useless to deny that the sufferings of the lost may even be interminable. Those sufferings are penalties incurred, not punishments inflicted. Nothing but real and disinterested goodness can make a man fit for Heaven, and it is impossible to conceive how the lost are to attain to such goodness. It is not necessary to deny absolutely that they may: nor is it necessary to deny that the pity of God may put an end to their sufferings and their existence together. But there is no trace of either of these ideas in the New Testament, and they are hard to reconcile with what we know of human nature. We seem compelled to think of ourselves as indestructible— unless indeed we are to perish like the beasts. That which lives on after death must (we feel) live on for ever. It would almost seem as if the Almighty in bestowing the awful gift of moral freedom had also bestowed the not less awful gift of unending existence. These are of course only ideas, intuitions, speculations, having no warranty in reason or experience—but they cannot be ignored.

The doctrine of annihilation will never find more than a lukewarm and hesitating acceptance even with those who might expect to profit from it most. That God should take the souls of the lost to pieces and use them up again in some other form is the dream of a poet; a dream which seems to stand out of any conceivable relation to human nature as we are conscious of it in ourselves, or as it stands revealed in Scripture. It is precisely the personality of the man, be he good or evil, which is for ever insisted on: a personality of which

he cannot rid himself and of which no power in heaven
or on earth can rid him : a personality in virtue of which
God Himself is bound to deal with him (in a certain
sense) upon a footing of equality. For although He be
omnipotent and we the creatures of His hand, yet will
He respect our moral freedom, and respect also (we are
obliged to think) our personal identity, so as not to destroy
or confuse it even for our own good.

Out of all these considerations there emerges therefore
the one certain conviction that God will never cease to
love the souls that are lost, will never fail to do His best
for them. Nay, we may be sure that as He can never
forget them in their misery, He must suffer with them
as long as they suffer themselves. Every father's heart
tells him it must be so. This is itself an unspeakable
consolation. It can no longer be said that the smoke
of hell blackens the gates of Heaven. The love of God
is vindicated : it is seen to be stronger than death, even
the death of the soul. The whole aspect of the case is
altered and cleared, as far as God is concerned.

But on the other hand the outer darkness of which
our Lord speaks is as dark as ever. Nothing can ever
take away the effect of His words, or make them less
suggestive of horror. Nor does what we know of human
nature and what we are obliged to feel about ourselves
give the least countenance to those pleasing anticipations
which commend themselves to so many because they *are*
pleasing.

The end of the matter is (as so often) an inability to
come to any certain conclusion. There are reasons of
the greatest weight which draw us in diametrically opposite
directions. It would be easy to give ourselves up to the
domination of one set or the other. To balance them
one against another, with any hope of a definite result,

is impossible. That God will always love the soul He made in His own likeness is certain. How far that soul, in its freedom and in its separate personality, can defy His love is the problem which we have no means of solving: only in this dreadful contest all the analogy of this life *is on the side of the soul*.

EXCURSUS IV.

W HEN we come to consider it, this is quite one of the most noteworthy features of that Kingdom. It stands out in clear relief against the strongly marked tendency of all theology to cover the whole ground of religious enquiry. That tendency is indeed so rooted in human nature, and falls in so naturally with the craving of the human mind, that it is unreasonable to find any fault with it. "Lord, and what shall this man do" rises instinctively to the lips. We cannot help wanting very much to know how the Kingdom is to deal, in the way of inclusion or exclusion, with all the people in whom we are interested. We expect an answer, and when we first perceive that no *authoritative* answer seems to be forthcoming, we are keenly disappointed, and cast about for any possibility of supplying so grievous a want. The history of religious speculation has been, to a very great extent, the history of attempts so to piece together and to expand and to interpret our Lord's teaching as to make it cover the whole field of human questioning. These attempts have been made in good faith, and with any amount of ingenuity and determination. If they have failed, it is because our Lord willed that they should, and so formulated His teaching as to make their ultimate success impossible. We may approach the subject very conveniently along either of the lines indicated in the previous notes. It goes without saying (in these days, at least) that if people hold to the dogma of the eternity of future punishment—for which there is of course so much to be said—they are bound to minimize the number of the lost. All writers on that side do, from Dr. Pusey to Principal Salmond. In order to comfort us, in order no doubt to make it tolerable to themselves, they set aside vast numbers of mankind as not coming into question, and other whole classes as being safe within the mercy of God. They assume generally that all Christian children will be saved, and commonly that all heathen children will be saved too; that in fine none will be lost who have not definitely chosen evil rather than good, and darkness rather than light. No one will quarrel with these assurances in themselves, but it must be emphatically said that they have no express declarations of Scripture on which to found themselves. They are mere deductions from what is taught about the character of the Divine Being. There is not a word in our Lord's teaching which throws any direct light upon the future of children dying before responsibility begins: nor can anyone even guess when responsibility *does* begin. Every single reference to the great division concerns grown people alone, and such grown people as have taken sides with Christ, or against Him. It is possible to suppose that the parable of the sheep and goats refers to the heathen exclusively, and to understand that disinterested kindness shown or not shown will be the only and decisive ground of eternal separation for them. Very few will be able to accept that view of the parable, and there is nothing else to appeal to. The case of children (and something like one half the population of the world dies in infancy or childhood) is not alluded to, and cannot be brought (except in an arbitrary way) under any rule laid down in Scripture. Two lines of demarcation

have been laid down and accepted. St. Augustine taught
—and Calvin followed him in teaching—that all children
were elect or non-elect according to the eternal predestination of God. The elect go to Heaven, the others to
Hell—eternally. The Roman Church first accepted this
teaching with a certain unwillingness, and then abandoned
it without saying so. Finally it declared that all infants
baptized go to Heaven, and all unbaptized to Hell.
Recent efforts to mitigate the horrors of "damnation" are
very creditable—but do not touch the doctrine itself. For
all men are born in sin, and are children of wrath by
nature, and nothing can bring them within the Kingdom
but spiritual regeneration, and that is only bestowed in
baptism. Perhaps there is no one that reads this book
that holds either of the views just mentioned. We do not
deny the great mystery of God's predestination : but we are
not going to believe that the Father of our Lord Jesus
Christ doomed from all eternity millions of babies to
eternal pain. Some of the best people in the world have
believed it, and we should only make ourselves contemptible by indulging in cheap and obvious invectives
against it : but we are not in the least likely to believe it
ourselves. We know quite well that no single being can
enter the Kingdom without being regenerate, and being
made partaker of the new Life which is in Christ : but we
are not going to believe that a baby soul is lost for ever
because the clergyman was five minutes too late to baptize
it. That again is held by some who show more love for
souls, whether adult or infant, than almost any others.
God forbid we should deride or flout their belief : but it
never can be ours. The obvious fact is that about the
future life of children, dying as such, the New Testament
says nothing. We have positively nothing to fall back
upon but our Lord's known attitude of graciousness

towards them. It is certain that He took them in His arms and blessed them without considering who or what they were, and without making any distinction amongst them : of such, He declared, was the Kingdom of Heaven. Now it is true that the Church, with a true and blessed insight, has seized with a triumphant gladness upon that one small incident and those few kind words. It is upon the strength of this alone that she baptizes all the little ones brought to her and declares of each and all that they are God's children and the heirs of His Kingdom. The Church interprets our Lord's mind as being equally gracious and generous towards *all* infants brought to Him in baptism, and so encourages us to have the same confidence with respect to those who are *not* brought. Our Lord only blessed—could only bless—those actually brought to Him : but the blessing they received was reflected upon the whole class to which they belonged.

But however true the insight which has led the Church to attach such a profound importance to that one little incident and those few gracious words, it remains the case that nothing can really be deduced from them save that our Lord loves *all* children, and would have them as near as possible to Himself. That leaves many questions untouched. God would have all men to be saved—but all men are not saved. It is a pardonable exaggeration to say of many children, as the Psalmist does, that as soon as they are born they go astray and speak lies. Many indeed are vicious as soon as they are anything at all. Our tender feeling for them is as often as not dependent upon the fact that we do not know what is really in them. The New Testament throws no direct light upon the future of children, dying. It is necessary to draw special attention to this, because the religious poetry and sentiment of the day is full of speculations, assertions, assumptions, which have no basis whatever in Scripture. The parables and other teachings of our Lord which concern the final issues of human life *deliberately leave the children entirely out of sight*, although they constitute half the human race. That alone is proof enough that it is not possible to make a consistent theological scheme out of our Lord's teaching about the future. In such a scheme, *e.g.*, it is entirely illegitimate to co-ordinate a general deduction from St. Mark x. 14 with a literal insistence upon St. Matthew xxv. 46.

Passing now to the case of the heathen, it is certain that they and the non-Christians still form the bulk of mankind, and there is no direct reference to their fate in our Lord's teaching. St. Paul indeed appears to teach that they will be judged by natural law, according to the witness of their own conscience. We accept that, not only on his authority, but as witnessed to by the general conscience and conviction of mankind. But that throws little or no light upon their *eternal* future. The more we reflect upon the way in which heathens *do* live, the more impossible does it become to divide them (in thought) into saved and lost. Here are two heathens. Both have lived in the twilight of heathen customs and superstitions, and have lived by what we call the light of nature. Both have practised the vices which were condoned *and* the virtues which were demanded by the moral code of their race. Within the very narrow range which custom and opinion left open, one has been a little more just, temperate, kindly, than the other. Is it conceivable that a difference so slight, so apparently superficial, should make the difference between eternal happiness and eternal misery? Is it in fact possible from a New Testament point of view to say anything about their future except that it will certainly be affected by whatever independent choice they may have made of virtue or vice? We have to remember that in the case of the *Christian* we have the grace of regeneration, of union with Christ, which goes deep down into the very centre of his being and profoundly affects him there. His outward conduct corresponds—slowly and imperfectly—but still corresponds. Even a small outward and visible difference may conceivably be the index to a tremendous change *within* which the eye of God can see. But confessedly there is nothing of the sort in the case of the heathen. It is only a little better or a little worse in the very unsatisfactory life which all heathens live. It is equally impossible to believe that the heathens generally go to Hell, *or* go to Heaven. They stand, as far as we can gather, out of any assignable relation to either. The New Testament gives us no more information about their future than about the future of children. It seems to be the fact that all our Lord's teaching about the final issues of life concerns itself only with a small minority of the race—with those, viz., who as adults are brought face to face with Himself and either accept or reject Him. For the rest we may and do *trust* Him who showed such affection for little children; we may and do *trust* Him who nurtureth the heathen, and everywhere fills their hearts with food and gladness; but as to the eternal future of children or heathen the New Testament tells us nothing definite, and it is quite useless for us to pretend to know. Avowedly there is no revelation on the subject but that in Scripture : and that is totally insufficient for any dogmatic purposes.

We turn now to another line of approach. We have called attention to the emphatic way in which the New Testament couples present suffering with future glory. Not that the suffering *purchases* the glory, but that the outward suffering is the test and witness of the loyalty, the earnestness, the whole-heartedness of the inward faith. Our Lord, in the Apocalypse, goes the length of saying that He would

have people either hot *or* cold, and of representing Himself as unable to tolerate the lukewarm. That does not
stand alone. In the Gospels He uniformly speaks of
salvation as a matter of grave difficulty. Men have to
strive to enter in at the strait gate; and consequently
there are not many to be found inside. Moreover "the
righteous" are in His teaching perfectly distinct and unmistakable. We know them at a glance. If in that other
world they are divided by a great gulf from the wicked, it
is only because they are so already in this world. In this
world the gulf is a moral and spiritual one, but it is a
veritable chasm. Now the ideal life everywhere depicted
in the New Testament, with its disinterestedness, its self-
abnegation, its necessity of being persecuted, its blessedness of suffering for Christ, never has been and is not now
lived by more than a few. *And it is just those few who are
invariably contemplated when our Lord speaks of Heaven.*
Is it conceivable that our Lord should ever say, "well
done, good and faithful servant" to the vast majority of
Christian people? The most that can be said for them is
that they are influenced to a certain extent by Christian
feelings, and that they are more or less sorry when they do
anything very wrong. In a hesitating, half-hearted, way
they choose what is good—provided always it does not cost
them too much. They genuinely feel the attractions of
Christ's religion, and yield to them when it does not mean
really giving up or striving. It seems equally impossible,
as we think of them, to apply to them either the bright
side or the dark side of our Lord's picture-language about
the final issues. We recoil with a certain sense of help-
lessness and hopelessness from the contemplation of the
subject as if our Lord's teaching, beautiful and inspiring as
it is, were out of touch with the actual Christianity of to-
day. And it seems best to come to that conclusion, how-

ever unwelcome it may be. Anything is better than dishonest dealing with His words, and they really are not
applicable to the great mass of Christians. The Heaven
of the New Testament is for the brave, the just, the pure,
the loving: for those who have seen the heavenly Vision
and have surrendered themselves heart and soul to it—or
rather to *Him*, not counting the cost, not holding their
lives dear, not seeking their own, not drawing back. It is
for such as have really taken up their cross and followed
Him and not denied His name for any threatenings or
blandishments of this world. Blessed and happy souls,
these, whose treasure is in Heaven, for whom to live is
Christ, and to die is gain. Blessed and happy, God's
elect, His chosen few, His secret ones, who have made the
great renunciation, who have learnt the one lesson worth
learning, who in earth's dark places walk with Christ in
white, and shed a light of Heaven around them—who shall
hereafter walk with Him in white, for they are worthy.
Blessed and happy; for this is the only life worth living,
a life perfect and balanced and free, beside which any
other life shows so poor, so paltry, so futile. But the rest
of us, who are half and half, who make compromises, who
admire but cannot bear to go all lengths, who pursue with
some ardour the consolations which the Gospel offers, but
evade the sacrifices and deprivations it asks for: what shall
He do with us? It is not possible to *imagine* what He
will do with us. To talk of Heaven, as if everyone should
be welcomed there who is not quite bad enough to be cast
into Hell, is to play with the solemnest words of our Lord.
He did not speak of such as we are: and we will not
flatter ourselves that He did.

The more then we study His teaching about the Future
Life, the more astonished we are to perceive how straitly
that teaching is circumscribed. It leaves altogether out of

account all the children, all the heathen, and all the indifferent sort of Christians. We may, if we like, say that
all these will go to Hell. Or we may say that all these will
go to Heaven. We are at perfect liberty to do either,
because there is in fact nothing to direct and therefore
nothing to hinder us. But to assert either, *on the strength
of our Lord's teaching*, is a fraud. For His own wise
purposes He restricted His view to those people in whose
life and death, in whose present conduct and future fate,
the great principles of His Kingdom are clearly and
emphatically exhibited and vindicated. He contemplated
those about whom we could make no mistake. All the
rest—the vast majority apparently—He passes over. We
cannot really do anything else but pass them over too.
Whatsoever is right He will give them : we have to be
content with that.

INDEX

Anabaptists, 73–5.
Antichrist, 215.
Antinomianism, 48.

Baptism of infants, 108, 230, 261.
Birds of the heaven, 68.
Bohemia, our Lord's relations to, 131, 171, 195.

Charity, glorification of, 200, 244.
Christ, mystical union with, 189; second coming of, 150–159, 214.
Christianity, hereditary character of, 104, 136, 142; sacramental and non-sacramental, 91–97.
Church, as the body of Christ, 57–68, 76.
Council of Jerusalem, decree of, 226.
Counter-reformation, 87–89.
Cross, word of the, 19–26, 39, 55.

Departed, teaching concerning the, 211.

Faith, salvation by, 93, 187, 237.
Fiction, modern, 132, 196.
Forgiveness, difficulties in the way of, 116, 118.

Garment, the wedding, 139, 143.
Gnosticism, 42–44.
God, Fatherhood of, 249, 253, 256.
Gospels, authority of, 12.

Heathen, 197, 262.
Hermas, Shepherd of, 211.

Intermediate state, 156.

Kingdom of Heaven, character of our Lord's teaching about, 3–5, 10, 79, 100, 141, 210, 218, 258, 266; limitations to our knowledge of, 29–32, 80, 110, 259–266; time relations of, 6–10.

Life, eternal, 147.
Lost, destiny of the, 206, 241–257.

Millennium, 238.
Man, nature of, 246, 255.
Manichæans, 50.
Money, use of, 176.
Mormons, 48.
Mystics, 81, 85, 89.

Needle's eye, 141, 227.
New Testament writers, intolerance of, 44–46.

Old Testament, doctrine of the future in, 146.

Parables, tempers inculcated not transactions intimated by, 100, 102, 112, 125, 171, 176.
Prediction, absence of definite, 11, 12, 214.
Prophecies, nature of our Lord's, 160, 214.

Renunciation, the great, 27, 97, 237, 240, 265.
Revelation, book of, 165, 215, 237; latter part of ch. vii., 235.
Rome, Church of, 65.

St. Anthony, 97.
St. Augustine, 30, 35, 106, 212, 260.
St. Brendan, 208.
St. James, Epistle of, 18.
St. Paul, universalism of, 244, 246.
St. Peter, character of, 121–123.
Suffering, necessity of, 234, 263.

Tertullian, words of, 54, 224.

Works, judgment by, 185, 191, 193.

Zulu, religious history of, 47.

INDEX TO PASSAGES OF SCRIPTURE

Matt. xvi. 25, 26, pp. 23-25, 168-
170 ; xiii. 3-8, 18-23, pp. 16-
32, 37-39 ; *ibid.* 24-30, 37-43,
pp. 34-51 ; *ibid.* 31, 32, pp. 52-
69 ; *ibid.* 33, pp. 70-76 ; *ibid.*
44, pp. 77-89 ; *ibid.* 45, 46, pp.
90-102 ; *ibid.* 47-50, pp. 103-
110 ; xviii. 23-35, pp. 111-120;
xix. 12, p. 27, *note ; ibid.* 23,
pp. 227-230; xx. 1-16, pp. 121-
128 ; xxi. 28-32, pp. 131-134;
ibid. 33-43, pp. 134-136 ; xxii.
2-14, pp. 137-144 ; xxiv., pp.
150, 162 ; xxv. 1-12, pp. 167-
173 ; *ibid.* 14-30, pp. 174-180;
ibid. 31-46, pp. 181-218, 244 ;
xxviii. 19, p. 199.

Mark iv. 3-8, 14-20, pp. 16-32 ;
ibid. 26-29, pp. 9, 17 ; *ibid.* 30-
32, pp. 52-69 ; x. 15, pp. 230-
233 ; xii. 26, p. 146.

Luke viii. 5-8, 11-15, pp. 16-32;
xiii. 18, 19, pp. 52-69 ; *ibid.*
20, 21, pp. 70-76 ; xvi. 19-26,
p. 157 ; *ibid.* 27-31, p. 138 ;
xvii. 21, pp. 219-223.

John iv. 48, p. 220; vi. 53, p. 92 ;
xi. 25, 26, p. 148.

Acts xv. 29, p. 226.

Rom. xiv. 17, pp. 114, 223-227.

1 Cor. iii. 13-15, p. 158 ; viii. 8-
13, p. 224 ; xii. 12 ff., p. 60;
xiii., p. 201.

Eph. iii. 21, p. 61 ; v. 23 ff., p.
62.

Phil. iii. 8, 9, p. 83 ; *ibid.* 17-21,
p. 25.

2 Thess. ii. 3-9, p. 215.

Rev. ii. 28, xxii. 16, p. 82 ; vii.
9 ff., p. 235; xx. 4-6, p. 238;
ibid. 12, p. 191.

PLYMOUTH
WILLIAM BRENDON AND SON, PRINTERS